Dedicated to my husband

Author's Note

Aside from my immediate family and some close friends, the names and other identifying characteristics of the persons included in this memoir have been changed. Despite the name changes, all the events are true.

Contents

Chapter 1 8
   Introduction 8

Chapter 2 15
   My family 15

Chapter 3 21
   Growing up 21

Chapter 4 36
   Wanting to get married 36

Chapter 5 39
   Discovering the lump in my breast 39

Chapter 6 53
   Spending time with friends 53

Chapter 7 59
   Spending more time with friends 59

Chapter 8 66
   No Insurance? 66

Chapter 9 71
   Beach therapy 71

Chapter 10 80
   Enjoying my job as a Recreational Therapist. 80

Chapter 11 91
   Pretending to be someone else. 91

Chapter 12 98
   Resolving the insurance problem. 98

Chapter 13 101
   Getting a second mammogram. 101

Chapter 14 106
   Meeting with the doctor....................................106

Chapter 15 114
   Trying to make surgery fun..................................114

Chapter 16 125
   Recovery 125

Chapter 17 130
   Radiation & chemotherapy................................130

Chapter 18 137
   Promises of adventure and marriage 137

Chapter 19 149
   Loss of appetite..149

Chapter 20 153
   Work & losing my hair 153

Chapter 21 167
   Relationships..167

Chapter 22 170
   Path to recovery 170

Chapter 22 176
   Drug-induced euphoria and trying to enjoy life 176

Chapter 23 182
   Love of children 182

Chapter 24 188
   "DES" 188

Chapter 25 192
   Letting go of the hair loss 192

Chapter 26 200
   New California job 200

Chapter 27 205
   Struggling with weight gain & low self-esteem 205

Chapter 28 211
   Valuing life—The Iraq War....................................211

Chapter 29 217
   Cherishing friends 217

Chapter 30 221
   Feeling better...221

Chapter 31 226
   Overcoming depression 226

Chapter 32 232
   Broken leg..232

Chapter 33	235
False hope	235
Chapter 34	239
Near death	239
Chapter 35	241
Care-free	241
Chapter 35	245
Signs of infertility	245
Chapter 36	254
Kiss ovaries goodby?	254
Chapter 37	256
Fostering a child	256
Chapter 38	265
Promised blessings	265
Chapter 39	271
Meeting my husband!	271
Chapter 40	277
Honeymoon	277
Chapter 41	279
Step-motherhood	279
Chapter 42	281
A new beginning & desires for children	281

Chapter 43	285
Battling infertility	285
Chapter 44	291
Fertility treatment	291
Chapter 45	297
Helping a friend with cancer	297
Chapter 46	303
Unexpected death	303
Chapter 47	306
God's perspective	306
Chapter 48	310
Taking care of friends	310
Chapter 49	311
Cancer returns?	311

Chapter 1

Introduction

Las Vegas lights on the strip sparkled in the somewhat cold December morning from my window at the Tahitian Village Resort. Early before sunrise, I looked at my phone; someone had called the day before. Since everyone was sleeping, I stepped out in the hall to keep from waking them and listened to my message. I had been expecting a call from the doctor. The results of my chest X-ray that I needed because of my bad cough and asthma should have been ready by now. The doctor had not called yet so I assumed all was fine. I really thought the tests would not be anything too concerning; but after I heard the tone of his voice as I listened to the message, I began to worry maybe it was more than just bronchitis.

"I have your Chest X-ray reports, and I would like to talk to you. Sorry, I did not get back to you sooner, but I just now got the reports. Please call me."

It was Christmas Eve when I got the message, and I tried to call him back as I went to work out at the gym. He was not there. He called me back when I was on the treadmill about 15 minutes later. I quickly answered the phone. His voice was solemn, and he spoke directly to the point.

"The X-ray is showing a dense nodule in the right lung. They are recommending a CT scan. Did you have cancer on the right side or both sides?"

"Just the right side, but I did have a lump removed before on the left, but it was not cancer."

"Yes, that explains the scaring they are seeing on the left side. The CT scan will need to be scheduled so they will be calling you. I would like to see you when you get back because the X-ray also shows bronchitis in the right lung."

I hung up the phone told my husband, who was with me at the gym, what he said. We both felt it would be nothing to worry about. I began to run hard and harder than I normally would have. I pushed beyond my physical capabilities as I thought of the possibility that my cancer had come back, but after 23 years, how could it? I began to cry; Bart came over, and I said,

"I am scared" (as I continued to run). "I am not scared to die but I want to take you with me."

"Just poison me, and then I can go too," he said half jokingly.

I knew he was actually sincerely wishing he could go with me if I were to go anywhere.

That day, Summit Health Imaging central scheduling called, and I scheduled the appointment for the CT scan for January 2nd. They would not be open until then. I decided I would not tell any family because I did not want to stress people out at Christmas.

After hearing this news, I tried to enjoy our trip, and we saw three great movies, Les Miserables, Life of Pi, and The Hobbit. We ended our trip by eating at the Wicked Spoon for my husband's birthday, sampling all kinds of wonderful foods, including crab, fruit tarts and delicious gelato; we drove home. It was a perfect way to end our vacation.

Then on December, 30th Sunday morning, I was reading about "dense nodules in the lung" on the Internet. At first when I read, I did not feel like I had much to worry about since it said dense nodules were very common. But then I read that if you were over age 50, the chance of nodules being cancerous was about 50%. I began to worry more and wanted to tell people to pray for me.

Although I had talked to my mom that night before, I hadn't told her anything about the medical tests. I now called my mom first and told her to please pray for me. She was getting ready for church and said she and my Dad would pray for me. I called all my brothers and sisters and Bart's family. I left a message for them because no one answered their phone. I called some of my good friends Sandy, Janet, and Carol and I told them to please pray for me.

That day at church, Bart and my home-teacher gave me a Priesthood Blessing of healing. In the blessing, the words were simple. He told me that Heavenly Father was aware of my condition and that through my faith I would again be restored to my full health. This was comforting to know. I told myself that I would put this in the Lord's hands, and He would fight the battle for me.

The next day, on New Year's Eve morning, I lay in bed pleading with God that it would not be cancer. I reflected on the words from my blessing and also from our Snowflake Stake president regarding what he said in Sunday school yesterday. "God will actually fight our battles for us if we let him." He was not speaking personally to me. He was making reference to the righteous King Hezekiah of the Jews about 700 BC. King Hezekiah was a great religious and political reformer. He stood up against the King of Assyria that threatened to come to war against them. At that time, King Hezekiah counseled with the prophet Isaiah. Isaiah prophesied the destruction of the Assyrians. Hezekiah went before the Lord and prayed for his people that they might not be overtaken by the King of Assyria. In 2 Kings 19 verses 32- 37 Hezekiah receives his answer from the Lord.

> 32 Therefore thus saith the LORD concerning the king of Assyria, He shall not come into this city, nor shoot an arrow there, nor come before it with shield, nor cast a bank against it.
>
> 33 By the way that he came, by the same shall he return, and shall not come into this city, saith the LORD.
>
> 34 For I will defend this city, to save it, for mine own sake, and for my servant David's sake.

> 35 And it came to pass that night, that the angel of the LORD went out, and smote in the camp of the Assyrians an hundred fourscore and five thousand: and when they arose early in the morning, behold, they *were* all dead corpses.
>
> 36 So Sennacherib king of Assyria departed, and went and returned, and dwelt at Nineveh.

I thought to myself again, when I read this as I did the first time I heard it in Sunday school class, "I can let Him fight my battle with cancer, if this is cancer."

Suddenly an intrusive thought came into my mind, "Is this because I tried to get pregnant by in vitro-fertilization in 2010?" But, I really thought it was the right thing to do because my patriarchal blessing says: "It will not be exceedingly difficult for you to bring children into the world." That part of my blessing has made me hang on to the hope that someday I would bring not just a child, but children into the world. So when the medical studies finally said that there was not the high risk that was originally thought for women with estrogen receptor positive breast cancer in getting pregnant after cancer, I believed this was my miracle I had been waiting for. I knew that a child or children were waiting for me. It was finally my chance to be a mother. And, now, not only do I not get to be a mother but my cancer comes back because I tried to have what so many women in my church call the most important calling in life, Motherhood. If this is the case, I don't understand.

Unless…hmmm, maybe it is God's plan for me to have cancer again, maybe it's a trial I need or others around me need. Maybe I need this to help increase my faith even more in my God, who I know will not forsake me. He will fight my battles if I let Him. I know he will carry me through every hardship in life. I know He is always with me and that He always has been. So, if I put my faith in Him, just like the Great King Hezekiah did, God can fight my battles too, And Angels will be there. I believe in Him! But of course, I hope the dense nodule is nothing, and if it is nothing, I will be grateful for that too.

Chapter 2

My family

I am a 55, soon to be 56 year old, LDS, woman who was married in the temple, and who has never had children of her own. I am a Breast cancer survivor of 23 years. I truly hope for a miracle that this dense nodule is not cancer. This is my story of surviving cancer and surviving life. I think the best place to start is at the beginning.

I was the third born of seven children to Randolph Ray Gibson and Mary Jeannette Jewett. My mom told me I was conceived in Texas. I guess that explains my fetish with cowgirl boots at a very young age. I think it was safe to say that I was the only child at elementary school wearing them faithfully each day to first grade and maybe the only first grader who wore them in all of Long Beach, California.

When I was growing up, we had a ranch in Nevada, and we would go there and ride our horses. This experience of living in our old ranch house for a few weeks each year added to my fantasy of being a cowgirl.

As I was saying, my parents raised seven children. Carla is the oldest. She was a runner-up for Top Ten College Girls in Glamour Magazine. She has always been a high achiever and was involved in student government in High School; she was student body president at Long Beach City College. She later went to Brigham Young University on a leadership scholarship and chaired the first BYU Women's conference while serving as the Associate Women's Student- body President. Whenever I attended the same college Carla had already attended, I became known as Carla's little sister and was given opportunities to serve in appointed leadership positions as a result of her being my sister. For example, I was appointed to be the Associated Women Student's Community Service Chairperson at LBCC, and I started a community service volunteer program that allowed students to volunteer in their possible career path so they could know whether or not they would really like that career. Later, when I followed her to BYU, I was able to serve on a committee for a women's conference, and I remember having lunch with some of the guest speakers including Camilla Kimball, wife of the former LDS prophet, Spencer W. Kimball. Carla has been a natural leader all her life, and I had many opportunities because of her.

Jane, a piano virtuoso, was the second child born. She was born with perfect pitch. She went on to get her Master's in Piano performance. She won the Gina Bachauer Award in college and performed as a guest performer with the Utah symphony. Thirty years later, after raising her severely Autistic son, she went back to compete, and with only one year of practice was one of the six finalists in the Sixth International Van Cliburn Piano Competition for Amateurs. She won the press jury award. As a result, she was featured in newspaper articles across the country. One reporter referred to her playing as "heavenly or angelic". Jane was born to be a musician. Growing up, I would hear a song on the radio that I liked, and I would ask Jane to play it; she would play the song without ever seeing a note.

As I attended the same school as Jane, teachers would look at me and ask me to sing a correct note—assuming I could do this like Jane. I would simply say, "Sorry, I am not Jane, and I think the piano can give you the note just fine." They also thought my GPA should be like hers, but it wasn't. In-fact, my parents were happy if I merely received a B or C grade.

My next sister is Carol Noel who was born on Christmas day. She is 2 years younger than me. She excelled in school, especially in music. Carol was born a natural sales woman. By the time she was out of High school, she was driving a cute sports car and making good money while going to college. Carol was the first sibling to get married and also had the first grandchild. Later, she sold advertizing for yellow pages, was always the top sales person in the nation, and won trips and all types of prizes from her natural talents. She alone raised two children from her first marriage. After remarrying, she had three more wonderful children. Carol has amazingly beautiful and talented children (as are all my nieces and nephews but, of course, I am not biased at all).

Two years later after Carol, Missy Margaret Jennie was born to my family; she was a talented softball player. She played on the Long Beach City College team, would sometimes play with my Dad's team, and it was even said that she could throw as powerfully as a man. I felt her strength once while trying to catch a ball she threw for my Sports Kinesiology class project. I was video-taping her throw to analyze for my class assignment. As I caught the ball, I broke my finger. It was merely a hairline fracture, so it did not stop me from playing in our city league softball playoff game. I just took a pain killer and played catcher that night. I can't remember if we won or lost, but I do remember playing with a broken finger. Missy sure could throw a ball hard and fast.

Missy studied nursing, became an RN, and works on a Pediatric cancer unit. She is married and has two wonderful children. The last child was recently adopted. She is a sweet baby girl.

Finally, the sixth and seventh children of my parents are boys. Doug is an intellectual jock and talented writer. He has always been a natural learner and great writer. He wrote for the college paper at BYU and then professionally while first living in Boston and then later (currently) as a newspaper editor in Utah. Doug is happily married and has four awesome children.

Dave is the youngest and he is adopted. He surfed when he was younger, likes to fish, and is married with two children. He is a wonderful family man, does an outstanding job at providing for his family, and has always been a hard worker. Dave has always excelled in all of his business endeavors. One of the jokes in our family is that he is the only one who did not get some college but now makes more than all of us.

All of my family members have had a great influence on my life, in many different ways. I think it is good that we are all very different in interests and lifestyles. No one wants to be a carbon copy of someone else. Do they?

Chapter 3

Growing up

As for me, Nancy, I loved dance, music and theater, but most of all, I really loved being around friends and having adventures. I enjoyed learning Polynesian dance. My friend, Sandy and I danced at many luaus. At one time, I even wanted to dance my way through college and possibly go to BYU-Hawaii while working at the Polynesian Culture Center in Laie, Oahu. It never happened. I guess it was not really meant to be—not part of the plan for me. I performed in the chorus of our high school musicals. Swimming also became an important aspect of my life. I became a pool life guard as well as a swim teacher and have since taught 500 or more children to swim.

Academics was not first priority for me. I think, I worried my mom the most because I seemed much more concerned with having fun and not so much concerned about planning for the future and for a career. Ironically enough, I am one of the sisters that worked my entire life and I've had a long productive career and even ended up with a Masters in Educational Counseling and a Teaching Certification after a

20 year career in Recreational Therapy with my BS degree from BYU. Somehow in-spite of myself and my fun-loving attitude toward life, I was able to accomplish some things.

I think the strong family values, standards, and expectations I grew up with helped me be motivated to make something of my life because, of course, I would have much rather followed the summer sun around the world and visit all the beaches I could.

If you were to describe my growing up years, you could say that it was a mix between Beach Boy songs, Mary Poppins, the Mormon Tabernacle Choir, and the original Gidget movie. I know, you might be saying that's an odd combination of influences.

Let me try to explain. My life was like a Beach boy song because I loved everything about the surf culture and wanted to be a part of it in any way I could but only if I could still keep my very high Mormon standards.

My life was like Mary Poppins because I thought of myself as someone who could tame the most unruly child and do it all with great love and a song in my heart. I babysat a lot. I was good at it! The kids all liked me because I was fun. Everyone thought, including me, that I would someday end up having at least 10 children.

Next, my life was like the Mormon Tabernacle Choir because of the youth choir I sang in at church when I was ages 13-16. Our choir sang all over California, and we had a few Utah performances too. Our choir director was a senior in high school. Our pianist was my sister, Jane, of course. While singing in our youth choir, I had some of my most sacred spiritual experiences. My favorite song was *The Spirit of God*. Here are the first two verses. This song had a very strong influence on me. It is a song about the restoration of the fullness of the gospel.

> The Spirit of God like a fire is burning!
> The latter-day glory begins to come forth;
> The visions and blessings of old are returning,
> And angels are coming to visit the earth.
> We'll sing and we'll shout with the armies of heaven,
> Hosanna, hosanna to God and the Lamb!
> Let glory to them in the highest be given,
> Henceforth and forever, Amen and amen!
>
> The Lord is extending the Saints' understanding,
> Restoring their judges and all as at first.
> The knowledge and power of God are expanding;
> The veil o'er the earth is beginning to burst.
> We'll sing and we'll shout with the armies of heaven,
> Hosanna, hosanna to God and the Lamb!

> Let glory to them in the highest be given,
> Henceforth and forever, Amen and amen!

Lastly, I was not that much like the Gidget character, but I did spend many of my growing up years at Beach parties and chasing surfer boys just as she did. I also think I was like Gidget because I could relate to her feelings of sometimes not being accepted as one of the crowd. After all, I was a Mormon girl, and I did not drink, smoke pot, or have sex before marriage; and since I'd never been married, yes, that meant that I was also a virgin and would remain so until I was married in the temple someday.

It was 1974, I was living near the beach in Southern California, and these were my standards. I was not the only one with high standards in those days. There were many other youth doing the same thing as me, adhering willingly to these same high standards and living in a world without such high standards in the Southern California surfer culture. There were differences, however, between me and some Mormons. I not only hung out with members of my church, but I also liked to talk and become friends with everyone, no matter what their faith or ethnical background was. After all, we are all God's children, right? This is how I thought people should be. As I chose to hang out with all kinds of people, at times it seemed awkward when I did not fit in with either group. Bottom line, even though I was more like my Mormon friends because we shared the same standards, I was not limited to what only members of my church were thinking, and I always felt like I could relate to more people than just those of the Mormon (LDS) faith. I always spoke openly about my beliefs to others outside my faith, and I was not afraid to share what I knew and believed to be true.

While I was growing up and later on as a young adult, I enjoyed learning about all kinds of people. I remember, for example, a conversation with a very nice surfer girl in my High school days, during the era of free sex that was before HIV and AIDS, I think it went like this.

> "You've never had sex before? I don't get it. Why are you doing this to yourself?" said the very nice surfer girl.
>
> I responded, "In my church, I have learned it is better to wait until you are married. I think that making love is something you should save for the person you love enough to commit to forever and for eternity." (I liked calling it "making love" because sex sounded so base, and it was not romantic enough for me.)

Surfer girl then said. "Wow that is like the opposite of me. When I go to a party and meet a guy, if I think I will see him again like at school or somewhere then I won't have sex with him because it might be too awkward to see him later, but if I know I'll never see him again then I'll do it."

I don't remember what I said after that. I think I was speechless and shocked, that someone who I really liked talking to had such a drastically different view of sex, or making love, than I did.

Now, Beach Boy song's had an important role in my life. They seemed to fulfill my idealistic fantasy of the surf culture. I can't explain why, but every time I heard a Beach boy song for the first time, I felt like I had heard it before and somehow it was a song about my life. For example, I remember dancing at the Mormon Youth dance for ages 14 to 18 to the song, "Surfer Girl." One night, since I had arrived at the dance, I had been flirting from afar by making some good eye contact and smiling with this tall lanky surfer boy with bushy blond hair and deep set eyes that looked right through me.

Flirting was an art for me. I don't know where I learned it. Maybe, it was old movies. Somehow I knew how to do it. It was all in the timing and the subtle but deliberate glances. It's great because it's a non-verbal language that can say so much more than words and at the same time you are not actually saying anything verbally so there is safety because there is no real commitment. A shy glance in his direction breaking away and then connecting again had a power to invite with no real invitation. Some might say it's like fishing. The lure is out there, but it takes someone to actually bite before you can make the catch. If they don't bite it's okay because there are always other fish in the sea.

I was very interested in boys from very early on. I remember purposely "acting" like I needed help on a night hike at 6th grade camp so the boys would hover around me and hold my hand to help me get across the creek.

Okay, so I was a little boy crazy, I admit. I once tried to count all the boys I ever liked in my life and finally gave up because I could not remember them all. I sometimes read my old journals, and as I read, I'd have to ask myself, "Who is that guy?" or I'd say to myself, "I completely forgot about that guy."

Anyway, back to the story, I had been flirting with this tall surfer guy all night, even when I was dancing with other guys, and he was dancing with other girls, but all the time we were still looking at each other. Finally, he asked me to dance and it was the slow song, Surfer Girl. He took my hand and led me out on the dance floor. He did not even ask me but just came and took my hand as if we both knew we were going to dance to that song on that night. I felt like there were a hundred butterflies flittering all at once in my stomach. I had achieved my goal to dance with him. As we were dancing, I felt a third hand rubbing my back. I looked around and it was the tall surfer guy's friend. He was dancing with a girl next to us and they were laughing because he had been rubbing my back for a while before I even noticed.

    I was a total romantic and craved romance and dreamed of falling in love with the right man. I received my Patriarchal blessing at age 14. This is a blessing given by a man called to be a Church Patriarch for the purpose of helping me receive inspiration from God about my life. The patriarch that gave me my blessing did not know me personally, yet he gave me inspired information to help me stay on course with God's plan for me. A patriarchal blessing is given to any member in the church that wants one. The patriarch is a man called of God that has been given Priesthood authority to give a special Patriarchal blessing of guidance and direction of your life pertaining to your future regarding one's gifts, talents, weaknesses and significant events. It can tell you things God has in store for you that will come true but only if you follow Christ and keep His commandments. I went with my parents to the patriarch's home. He told me many things about my life, and it was recorded and later typed up and mailed to me for my personal use. I always loved the counsel, revelation and advice I received that day, and I read my blessing often.

In my Patriarchal blessing there was counsel for me about dating. My parents were strict about dating. I could not date until I was 16 years (which is common in the Mormon Church). My parents did not allow me to date people who did not belong to my church until I was 18. I did have many friends at school that asked me out, and I had to tell them I could not go out with them. Instead my High School year's social life prior to age 16 was mostly attending Southern California church dances and non-drinking parties by friends at church.

One night, I went to a Long Beach dance and there was a surfer guy that came with his Mormon friend to the dance. I was very attracted to him. He asked me to dance and he took my phone number. I was 17; he was 20. He had long sun bleached hair and sun-tanned face with a small sun burned nose from surfing all day. He was about 5'8" and had a very kind face with a sparkling smile. He had just gotten back from a surf trip for 3 months in Mexico. He was my first real boyfriend that could actually come and pick me up and drive me on a real date. There was only one problem, my parents could not know because I was not allowed to date non-members. He was Catholic.

At first, I dated him by having him pick me up at a friend's house; he did not know that I was hiding him from my parents. I did not want him to know that I was not allowed to go out with him. We dated about one wonderful month before I finally told him that I was dating him behind their back. He immediately told me that I had to tell them or we could not date anymore. I told him I did not want them to know because I had lied to them, would lose their trust, and would get in trouble. Maybe grounded forever. Who knows?

He was a good person and taught me how to love. Even though, at first, I think I loved him more than he loved me, and later, after I had turned 18, and could date him, I dated him again, but we broke up again. Somehow, we met each other again and again throughout my single years and dated some more. I dare say he loved me more than I loved him in the end. He was a true Christian man and never tried to take advantage of me. I still cherish the memories. Years later, at age 27, when I went on my mission to Hong Kong, he wrote me and even sent me money to help support my mission.

In my growing up years, my favorite dances were the Torrance dances. I would spend the day at Huntington Beach and get that sun glowed face for the dance. I'd be in the water body-surfing all day and then go home and take my time getting ready for the dance. I would wash my hair and blow-dry it with my head hanging down to get more body and fullness in my hair. I wore my favorite pink medium length skirt—short but not too short. I always felt very pretty and enjoyed all the attention I received at the dances. We were known as the Long Beach girls. We made many friends there and attended many parties, dances, and missionary farewell sacrament meetings there.

Somehow, because my mom was good friends with our Bishop, who worked for the church education department, I was accepted to BYU, but on an academic probation. I had to take a class called "Effective Study Habits." It actually taught me how to study, and I had never learned how to study for tests. At BYU, I met many wonderful new friends that I would be friends with forever. It was interesting to get to know all the different people there. They would tell stories about how their parents met at BYU many years ago. I would tell them my parent's story which was quite different than their parent's stories.

Well, it all started, I would say, when my mom who had been raised in foster homes and orphanages in Los Angeles decided that she wanted to run away at age 14. She told me she closed her eyes and put her finger on a map. She opened her eyes and it was directly on St. George Utah. She had enough money to buy a bus ticket there. When she got off the bus, she went to the motel owner and lied about her age and asked for a job as a maid. The owner, Mr. Dewsnip, invited her home to meet his family. She lived there for a few days and she learned about the gospel of Jesus Christ from this wonderful family. When I was growing up we called them Grandma and Grandpa, and we visited them each time we passed through St George, Utah when we drove to our ranch in Nevada. Eventually my mom came back to Los Angeles, and found the nearest LDS chapel, and she went into Bishop Adam's office and told him she wanted to be baptized. She was in high school at the time (had skipped 2 grades because she was so smart).

My mother met my dad the year she would graduate from High school, at age 16! She was swimming across the street with a friend, where he was playing baseball on the Navy base. My dad had played in the minor leagues of professional baseball out of high school but then went into the Navy during the Korean War. He was from Alabama and had not known about the Church there. My parents met that day through friends. My mom would not give her phone number to my dad, but my mom's friend gave it to him and they were married before her 17th birthday. After they were married, he left on the ship and his best friend on the ship gave him a Book of Mormon to read; he was soon baptized in Japan. They were later sealed ("married for eternity" not just "until death do us part") in the St. George temple. My dad later wrote about the meeting of my mother in his personal history.

> "It was during this time that I met my wife, Mary. We were playing in a baseball tournament at the Long Beach Navy base. All the ships that had baseball teams were playing in this tournament which went all week. There were teams from cruisers, battleships, aircraft carriers and other types of ships. Usually the better teams were from the larger ships because there were more men to pick from. Our ship the USS Rochester and was not the biggest, but we won the tournament that week.
>
> I can remember very well the feeling I had when I first saw Mary. I had seen many pretty girls before and they never affected me that way. I had a very strong feeling that I needed to get to know her. I didn't realize at that time what was prompting me to meet her. But with the knowledge that I have now of how the spirit of the Lord works, I know that it was the Holy Ghost prompting me to get to know her.
>
> I asked her for her phone number, but she would not give it to me; but I asked her friend for it and she gave it to me. I called her that night and we talked for a long time, and she agreed to go to the movie with me."

I always enjoyed telling this story to all my roommates and friends at BYU because no one had a story like that one.

Always looking for an adventure and meeting as many different kinds of people as I could, I bravely went forth into my unknown world seeking answers and direction daily through my prayers and hoping to meet the man of my dreams.

With many dreams in my heart for the future but few plans for those things to happen, I casually went on with my determination to go to as many beaches and ski as many different mountains as I could in a lifetime, and I fully expected to meet the man of my dreams somewhere along the way. Years later, still having not met him, I kept on believing it would happen someday.

Me during my BYU days

Chapter 4

Wanting to get married

On January 15th 1989 I wrote in my journal the following.

Dear Journal,

Well, soon I will be 32 this year. Do you know what? Sometimes that is very depressing to me. You know I feel so vulnerable. I know that I am vulnerable. I guess I want to believe so badly that some guy will love me and that I will deserve a good faithful man. I want to believe in my Patriarchal blessing. My patriarchal blessing has been a source of strength to me all my life, but sometimes I doubt that some of the things will ever happen, such as, finding the man that I will marry. Sometimes I think I should deal in what is being offered. I feel fearful to wait for the right person because I don't want to live any longer alone and insecure. Then, I am fearful to go against what I have always believed or hoped for. I hoped I would marry someone who could help me have what I need right now and that is love and security.

Financially, I'm not doing well. Somehow I got myself into debt, and I am not making lots of money. In fact, I am barely making it here in Park City, Utah. I have a 2nd job and another part time 3rd job too. I am depressed because I can barely pay my bills. I pay my tithing too. I am working hard too. Then Adam tells me on New Year's Eve that he will pay my way home to California, pay to move everything home, and pay off my debts too. I do love him, and yet I just can't let him do this because I don't believe he is right for me. I just don't trust him. He is so different than me. Yet sometimes I feel angry at Heavenly Father because here I am trying to do what is right, yet I am being tempted to just marry Adam. I want to, but I am scared he won't be a faithful and a good husband, or that he will never join the church. He is very rich, and I would love to have that kind of financial security to just play and travel like he does. He is sweet, but he is not very reliable, yet maybe he would be different if I could or would commit myself to him. I wish I lived in California so I would be making more money, and I would know more clearly if Adam was truly in love with me like he says he is. Yet I am afraid that if I was there he would be a situation for me that would be stronger than I am. I would be sacrificing a lot of my beliefs for him, yet I do love him so I feel like I should sacrifice for him. Life is tough sometimes. I miss having good friends I can talk to and rely on. I miss Jennifer. She is my best friend, and it is hard giving that up. I am happy she is serving a mission right now. Well, I guess when I finally get paid in the next week or so I will feel better to have money to pay my bills. I have not talked to Adam since last Wednesday, and it was just for a minute so I do miss him a lot. I need some good friends. I wish I could enjoy life more consistently. Just yesterday, I was a lot happier skiing, yet I was lonely too. I need a good friend to keep me happy. I do have lots of friends in California. I have met some very good friends here too; the new friend I like best is Sherry. She is a very high class person with lots of wisdom, and we get along really well. We enjoy skiing together. She also really appreciates my friendship too. I like her! Well, enough of this for now. I will write more at a later time. Tomorrow is another busy day. Lots of work and little money! My car is also breaking down.

That's all for now   Nancy

Chapter 5
Eight months later...

Discovering the lump in my breast

The speed limit was 65 mph on Interstate 80, but if the highway is empty, most people go 75 or 80 mph. At least that is what I did. We were probably going somewhere between 75 and 80 mph. We were anxious to arrive, since we only had approximately 800 or more miles to go. I was traveling with my niece-in-law, Monica and her friend Amy. Monica and Amy were both 17, and I was 32. We were excited to get away for 10 days to play along the coast, from San Francisco to Mexico, when I looked in my mirror to see a white car with flashing lights, a highway patrol car.

"Great, we're getting pulled over," I said. "Please hand me my purse. Let's pray we don't get a ticket. This is not the way to start out a vacation."

The officer looked like a nice Utah family man. "Good morning. Where are you headed?" he said, in a cheerful-yet-stern voice that only a highway patrolman is accustomed to.

"San Francisco."

"Where are you coming from?" he said as his eyes scanned the inside of the Toyota Tercel and all of our belongings.

"We live in Salt Lake and Park City," I replied in the most respectful voice I could muster.

"May I have your driver's license and registration, please?" the officer said.

"Yes, sir," I said and handed it to him.

He walked back to his car.

"He seems nice enough. I hope he doesn't give us a ticket," said, Monica.

The officer returned promptly and said, "I am not going to give you a ticket this time—just a warning. Please slow down. The speed limit here is 65. Drive safely, and have a good day."

"Thank you, officer. We will!"

And he left.

"Whew! Can you believe it? I am so lucky," I said to my friends. "I can't believe I almost always get a warning. That is my second warning in the last three months. I am the luckiest girl in the world!"

We pulled back onto the deserted highway and began the rest of the long drive-this time at 65 miles per hour. The long, stretching highway looked like a pathway of desolate, never-ending boredom at 65 mph. We had exhausted our supply of cassette tapes during the first two hours of the trip, and now we were not getting any radio stations either. So we invented a game called "Name That Tune on the Car Horn." We suddenly came alive as we challenged our minds with the monotone sounds of the rhythm of "Jingle Bells" then on to the song "Somebody" by Depeche Mode. We continued the game with a few more songs before we went back to the tapes we had brought with us. We enjoyed the sounds of Midnight Oil, Depeche Mode and some Reggae bands-Jimmy Cliff, Third World, and UB40.

We were about to have about as much fun as one can conjure up, vacationing along the coast from San Francisco to Mexico. We planned to take Highway 1 whenever we could and stop whenever we felt like it to swim and body surf along the way.

The long drive was worth it though because Southern California was where I had grown up. After college, I used to move back and forth from California to the Utah, changing jobs whenever I missed the mountains or the beach. I guess I was not sure where I belonged. For myself, this road trip was just one of many attempts to have as much fun and excitement as a single 32-year-old ever wanted or, in my way of thinking, expected to have. If work permitted, the money was there, and I had friends to enjoy the time with, then there was no question about it: Life was meant to be fun. It was definitely time for a vacation, and the excitement had just begun for Monica, Amy, and I.

As I listened to the music, my thoughts kept going back to the lump I had found in my right breast. Monica and Amy were talking about the guys they were leaving behind and the stories they would tell when they returned from their adventures. I broke into the conversation with an announcement:

"Did I tell you that I have a lump in my breast? I am sure it is nothing, but I will get it checked when I get home."

Monica looked confused and began questioning me. "No you didn't tell me. You mean like a cancer lump?"

"No I am sure it is nothing because I don't feel sick." I replied.

"Just the same you better see a doctor." Monica said in a parental sounding voice.

"What does it feel like?" asked Amy.

"A lump" I jested.

"That explains a lot." Monica sarcastically responded putting in a Depeche Mode tape and then taking it out again to put in Midnight Oil.

I went on to explain to them, "A few weeks ago, I watched a television special about Anne Jillian's experience with breast cancer. At the end of it, there was a demonstration of how to do a breast self-exam, so I tried it. I probably wouldn't have watched it or tried the exam, but a few months before, I had taken a test in a magazine to measure my risks for breast cancer. I had thought that my score would be very low with my healthy lifestyle. The questions asked if you drank alcohol, used drugs, ate a high-fat diet, and were sexually active. I believed that I would be at a very low risk. However, one question asked if your mother had taken DES when she was pregnant with you, a drug prescribed in the 1950s to help prevent miscarriages, which I answered yes to. That one "yes" put me in the 80 percentile bracket for my chance of getting breast cancer, according to this test. The doctors had always told me that because of the DES, I could get vaginal or cervical cancer in my late teens, and I had always been checked for it and never had anything abnormal. Now at age 32, I am supposedly not at such a great risk anymore." "I always get regular check-ups," I told them as they listened intently not knowing what to say.

I continued on, "Although, it has been at least two years since I have been to a doctor. I never get sick, so I just don't go. I am not really worried-that test wasn't even that valid. It's not like it was in a medical magazine; it was just some women's magazine! Besides, what are the chances that someone who has never done a breast exam before could find her own lump the first time?"

Monica and Amy, listening, seemed to feel the same way—that the lump couldn't be anything to worry about. Why worry? We didn't need to worry because we were about to embark on an extremely fun vacation. We planned on spending lots of time at the beach, meeting new friends, and visiting old friends along the way.

I said enthusiastically, "Hey Monica put on Jimmy Cliff's Many River's to Cross." I love that song, it's my life.

My thoughts went back to just before I had left to pick up Monica and Amy to leave. I was sitting in my mom's living room in the blue-flowered chair, telling my mom and sister, Missy, who is a nurse, that I had a lump in my breast.

I asked Missy "You want to feel it?"

She looked at me as if I was crazy and finally agreed to feel it after I insisted. Grabbing her hand, I pulled up my shirt and placed her hand on my right breast on the spot where I had felt the lump.

Missy looked at my Mom and said, "Hey, she does have a lump."

My mother, looking mildly bewildered and worried, said, "Have you seen a doctor?"

I quickly told her, "I will, later. I am sure it is nothing."

In my thoughts, during the long drive, I continued to reassure myself, whenever my thoughts drifted back to the lump, that there was nothing to worry about. I had never been sick a day in my life. I had never even had broken bones or surgeries except a tonsillectomy when I was three. Nor, had I spent the night in a hospital for any reason. There is nothing to worry about. I am sure of it, I thought to myself. I knew I was fine, so I quickly went back to thinking about the men I hoped to see in California. There was one in San Francisco and a couple in Long Beach. I always tried to have at least two men if not more to think about so that if one flaked out, there was always another one. Monica and Amy shared this philosophy. We were always thinking about the men in our lives or, the men not in our lives that we wished were.

At the time, I was 32 years old, single, and had never been married. Not a big deal in the rest of the world but in the Mormon culture, it was a big deal. I was looking for the right guy. Some in my family thought I was avoiding commitment and they thought I had a fear of real intimacy. When they talked like that to me, I disagreed. They had no idea how much I craved real intimacy.

Amy, me and Monica at Belmont Shores, Long Beach

I was living in Park City, Utah, in a house with three other roommates. I had recently starting working as a recreational therapist at a Children's Hospital Residential Treatment Center for emotionally disturbed latency-age children. I loved my career, and was finally making good money again but mostly I just liked to play and have fun. I am sure now my love for playing and having fun was in part a distraction or coping mechanism that I needed to deal with my loneliness. I had always been a person that was very social and liked having friends around. Even when I was only 14 years old I became best friends with Sandy Faulkner, when we first met.

Sandy and I age 18

We did everything together all through our first few college years and then we took different paths. I think we both knew no matter what we would always be friends though.

Monica was 17 years old and lived at home with her mother and her brothers and sisters. She was enjoying her last year of high school but was getting bored with the same old things. Amy her friend was also 17, also living at home. And now we were off on a road trip looking for some new and exciting things to do before the summer was over.

For us, this vacation promised to be an escape from our everyday Utah lives and a great opportunity to expand our repertoire of life experiences.

When I first met Monica, I was in college when her Uncle Lanny married my oldest sister, Carla. She was a little girl back then. I didn't get to know Monica too well until I had graduated from college. After college and my mission, I was working in California. Whenever I came to Utah from California to go skiing, I would end up with a car full of 14-year-old girls (Monica and friends) heading up the canyon to ski for the day at Alta. Monica also had visited me in California before.

More recently during the last year, while I had lived in Park City, she had brought several friends up for the weekend to my studio apartment at Treasure Mountain Inn on Historic Main Street before I had moved into the house with my roommates. She was a good friend, despite our age difference.

Amy had visited me with Monica several times and had skied with us before. She and Monica were best friends during their senior year. Amy had the look of a cover girl on the Seventeen Magazine. Monica's looks were more sophisticated; she was more suited to being a cover girl on a Vogue Magazine. I myself looked more like a typical California girl with my sun-streaked hair and tanned skin.

Chapter 6

Spending time with friends

The first night we spent in a Motel 6. After driving so long, we could not drive any further and needed to sleep. We woke up early to get on the road.

"Life is excellent, and we are on our way for dim sum in San Fran's Chinatown, shrimp cocktail and sourdough bread at Fisherman's Wharf and playing on the coast all the way to Mexico." I said to my friends as we headed back on the road again.

Each day of our vacation proved to be another fun adventure. We ate dim sum in Chinatown for breakfast as planned, and I spoke some Chinese with the Chinese locals. I had served a mission in Hong Kong just 3 years before, and my Chinese was still pretty good. Later, I enjoyed my favorite sourdough bread at Fisherman's Wharf and some shrimp cocktail for lunch.

Just south of San Francisco at a beach called Rockaway Beach, we met some cute guys in a rock band. Eddie and his rock-n-roll surf buddies were just hanging out at the beach—we discovered quite by accident. We talked to them on the beach that day for an hour or so and they wanted us to go to their place, "The Beach Shack," as they called it, so they could play their music for us. I myself was tempted to spend some time with Eddie and the band. They were college grads, musicians, and surf bums, and they looked fun. But, as the older of my two traveling companions, I felt I had to protect my younger friends. I whispered to Amy,

"Did you see the way Eddie was looking at you on the beach today?"

I continued to warn her,

"Who knows what he has in mind for you Amy?"

So we told them goodbye and headed further South down the coast to 17-Mile Drive along the coast of Monterey and Carmel enjoying the sights along the way.

Later in the day, as we headed toward Big Sur on Highway 1, we stopped to call Rick. He was a friend I met from church in Park City. He was good friends with my friend, Kevin, in Park City. Rick now lived in a house in San

Simeon, north of San Luis Obispo. We asked him if we could spend the night at his place. We were lucky—he was home and welcomed us. We were very tired and were glad to be able to have a place to sleep and to see Rick's loveable face again.

On the way to his house, the fog was thick on the coast, and the winding roads made us slow down to a crawl, with hardly any visibility to speak of. The only sight that was visible through the intense fog on the scenic route was the stretching arms of light rays that reached out from the 90-year-old lighthouse, lighting up the cliffs of the hundred-foot drop-off onto the rocky coast below.

Yet we arrived safely at Rick's house at the late hour of 2 a.m. and he was waiting for us. Rick greeted us and said,
"Good timing, my girlfriend just left to go home. She stopped by without notice and brought me some dinner," he said with a smile.
"She knew I had to work late, and I didn't have time to go out and get something. I did not tell her you were coming because I think she is the jealous type. She would not be happy if you had showed up when she was here, but if you did, I had a plan. I planned to act surprised to see you. But, I

am glad you came late so I didn't have to explain why there were three girls in my house spending the night."

We started unloading our stuff from the car. Rick yelled to us as we were gathering our things.

"Hey wait a minute. I forgot to tell you something. She will be calling any minute to tell me she made it home alright because she lives about an hour away, so I am asking you to please be completely quiet when she calls. Got it?"

"No problem, we can be quiet."

We were so tired that everything seemed funny. Rick was the kind of guy who made you laugh with his facial expressions and goofy sense of humor. We were making a bed on the chair and the couch when the phone rang. Rick answered it. As he spoke to his girlfriend, we pulled out the hideaway bed, and it creaked loudly. We all looked at each other, and Amy started to laugh. I quickly put my hand over her mouth. We were all trying to keep from laughing. Next, Monica flipped the sheet into the air across the couch while she was making the bed it made a swooshing sound, and again we started to laugh.

"Oh, um what noise?" Rick was saying into the phone. "That was the cat. That darn cat is always causing problems."

We somehow managed to keep from laughing out loud until Rick said good bye to his girlfriend and promised her they would go out the next night.

Rick came out to say good night and apologized that he couldn't stay up later because he had to get up early the next morning. That was okay with us because we were very tired, too. We tried to go to sleep, but with much difficulty. Just as we were about to fall asleep, the cat would jump across the bed as if he wanted us to give his couch back to him. After being pounced on over and over again, we finally nicknamed him Killer Cat but somehow finally we did fall asleep.

When we awoke, Rick was already gone. He had left us a note with his work number and in the note he said, please come and stay at his house on our way back home and to please call if we were planning to come back. We knew we weren't coming back that way, so we went to the store and bought some ingredients for chocolate chip cookies and homemade bread for him. We rapidly made the bread and left it on the counter to cool. Since he likes to eat the dough, we left the cookie dough in the fridge. We quickly signed a thank you note, and we were on our way.

That day, we tried to stay as close as we could to the coast. We lay out on the beach for a couple of hours to catch some rays at San Luis Obispo near the pier. Somewhere near Lompoc, we couldn't get close to the ocean anymore because of some military training grounds, and as we tried to find the beach we ended up lost for a while. We found a Jack in the Box in Lompoc, ate lunch there, and then got directions back to the highway.

Later that day in Malibu, we ate at Jack in the Box again. I liked their egg rolls and their onion rings too. All along we stopped several times to swim in the ocean whenever we felt like it. Everything was beautiful to me as we drove down the coast. This was pure relaxation.

Chapter 7

Spending more time with friends

After a long drive, we ended up at Huntington Beach, sitting in the sand, and watching the waves and the sun going down. My mind wandered, and I began thinking about a guy I had dated quite a bit in the spring before I moved to Utah. He was about 10 years younger than me.

Wherever I went, I seemed to attract the younger guys, and that is who usually asked me out. This same guy, Adam, had called me a few times while I was in Utah, asking me to move back to California. He even said he would pay for the move. I had really enjoyed my time with him, and I loved being with him. I found out later he was a major player and was full of lines and lies—at least that is what the girl said that answered the phone at his house one day when I called from Utah. I believed her.

I had liked him because he was fun to be with, but something always told me not to trust him so I knew it was good when I moved far away from him. He was one of those guys who used the words "I love you" to try to convince you that he was sincere. Being a single 32 year old woman, I often felt lonely, and it felt good to have someone say I was beautiful and to make a big deal over me, as he did. But he lied to me a lot and said the same things to other women besides me. He even pretended to be interested in my church, and he did his homework in the Mormon faith to keep up the lie, reading parts of the Book of Mormon so he could ask me realistic questions. This guy knew how to make a woman feel special. In fact, I think making women feel special was an art for him. My desire to be loved left me vulnerable to these types of dangers in dating.

The thing that had initially intrigued me about him was how he quoted Longfellow's "The Secret of the Sea" on the beach to me the second time we met.

> Ah! What pleasant visions haunt me
> as I gaze upon the sea!
> All the old romantic legends,
> All my dreams, come back to me.

How could he know that it was one of my favorite Longfellow poems? He had just met me the week before. Okay, so I was blinded by my love for a Longfellow poem, and he was feeding my under-nourished ego. Heaven only knows that it wasn't his looks. He really wasn't very attractive at all—just fun to be with.

Here I was minding my own business, enjoying my vacation, and remembering the fun times with him and the laughs we had together, and out of the blue, I see him coming out of the water! I watched him kneel down on the sand and put away his board in its cover. In a moment of weakness, I called his name, and he looked up and smiled at me. He came over as if we had never parted, and we sat on the beach and talked for a while. Monica and Amy took a walk down to Jack-in-the-Box. I told him all the same things I had said on the phone, such as how I felt about his dishonesty, but this time I tried to say it better yet still did not say all I really needed to say or all that I should have said to him. But I did say I was really angry about all the lies he had told me. He listened for about 30 minutes and then he asked me out—I just laughed at him. It felt good. I told him I wanted the pictures of me I had given him back, so he gave me his new phone number to call. He didn't ask for his pictures of himself back. (It was a good thing because I had already ripped them up.)

I saw Amy and Monica coming back, so I told him I had to leave. He then grabbed me and kissed me. I let him—there was a part of him I was attracted to. As Amy and Monica came back, he walked us to the car. We left him standing there, waving, as we drove off.

Next, we went to my friends, the Jensen family. I had known the Jenson family from church, and I used to baby-sit for them when I was teenager. We knocked on the door without any prior notice and asked them if we could use their shower. They laughed at us and told us to come in. They had two boys about the same age as Monica and Amy. The boys were already planning to take them to a movie with a group of friends.

They ordered a pizza for us, and then Amy and Monica went to a movie. I stayed home with the parents, Larry and Kathy, and their younger daughter, Suzi. I also called Adam's number a few times to try to get my pictures back, but he wasn't home or was avoiding me.

They all came back from the movies, and then they asked if I wanted to go with them to the grunion run. Grunions are small fish that come ashore in Southern California at certain times late at night. People bring buckets to gather them up, and they can be used for food or bait. I was wondering if there would really be any grunion, because while I was growing up, the grunion run was something you always used as an excuse to get to go the beach late at night, so I asked, "Are the grunion really running?" The boys told me there really were going to be grunion, so we decided to go.

We sat in the moonlight on the sand. I enjoyed watching the people gather up the fish in their buckets and thought how resourceful they were to be there. Some of them looked quite poor, and I felt sad to see them in this rich country we live in. I was reminded of how sheltered I am in my comfortable existence.

The next morning, we were off to San Diego to visit my good friend, Carol Harvey Stewart. She had recently married Kevin. Carol and I had met in Hong Kong and we had become good friends. She was my mission trainer in Hong Kong; my first companion. We called mission trainers "our mission moms." After we left Hong Kong, she had moved to California from Canada to work as a nanny for a movie director in Malibu. Later she lived in San Diego, also working as a nanny.

During her single years, we went to a lot of dances and beach parties together. When she moved to San Diego after I moved to Utah, there she met her husband, Kevin, while he was going to school at the University of California-San

Diego and playing basketball there. It was always so fun to see her again.

Carol Harvey Stewart and I on the way to Rosarito Beach

The next day, Carol went with us to Mexico. In Mexico, we went to Rosarito Beach, Ensenada, and La Bufadora. We bought Chanel No. 5 perfume (my favorite) and some turquoise, silver, mother of pearl, and abalone dangling earrings. We ate churros at La Bufadora—the best churros I have ever had. We also bought some Mexican vanilla for my mom to use in her pound cakes.

We also enjoyed trying to speak Spanish with the locals. It was especially funny because Carol and I both kept accidently speaking Chinese when we tried to use our Spanish. I always had a good time with Carol because of all we had been through in Hong Kong and after our Mission.

After the fun in Mexico and eating our share of fish tacos, we said good bye to Carol and we went back to another friend's house in Long Beach. We were invited to stay and eat at the Santos's house. Joe and Helen Santos had always been like family and yet treated us as if we were royalty, always bringing out their best china dishes to serve us, and we would eat until we couldn't think of eating another bite.

Helen Santos was the epitome of Southern hospitality. It was really more than that. She had a gift to make you feel so loved. She had always loved me since I was a little girl, and I could feel her love.

After a few more days of swimming, dancing, and seeing old friends, it was time to head home. The vacation had kept my mind off the lump. I honestly did not think that I could have cancer. "No, not me," I thought to myself. "I am not a sick kind of person. After all, I am the luckiest girl in the whole world!"

Chapter 8

No Insurance?

I had been avoiding my annual gynecological exam. I had started early with my exams when I hit puberty because I was a DES baby. Since I was about 14 years old, I had received one each year from my mom's OB/GYN. I had dreaded those painful examinations and felt humiliated because I would jump all over the place on the examining table when the doctor stuck those cold steel instruments up me to make sure there was no cancer.

My mother had been very cautious to make sure nothing had happened from the DES; she had taken me in faithfully for my exams, as recommended, every six months. Now that I was an adult, I was not as exact with my appointments. I had sometimes gone two or more years without seeing a doctor.

I called a doctor for a routine pap smear. The day of the appointment, at the doctor's office, I found out that I did not have insurance. I was angry because I thought I did—since I had just started a new job at the Hospital where I worked.

"What do you mean my name is not showing up? I work full time so I have insurance. Please look again."

She said, "Would you like to use my phone to call HR and see what the problem is?"

"Yes. I would, thank you!" I replied.

When I called HR they told me I was currently receiving flex dollars, and I did not have insurance but could sign up at the next available open enrollment in January. Well that was in about 3 more months. I did not tell the nurse about the lump because I really did not think it was anything, and I had almost forgotten about it again. I left without seeing the doctor that day.

Now, I was trying to figure out why I was getting flex dollars. I did not remember signing up for flex dollars. Later, after talking to Human Resources, I found out that I had not filled out all of the necessary paperwork for my benefits at the hospital wide orientation. The day I was supposed to go to the orientation for my specific department, my boss, the director of the psychiatric residential treatment facility where I worked, had asked me to work with the patients rather than go to the orientation because they were short-staffed. This was a never-ending problem in health care—particularly in psychiatric facilities-probably because of the shortage of reimbursement from insurance companies.

I finally found out that since I had not finished the necessary paperwork to be enrolled to receive my medical insurance, I started receiving flex dollars by default. I had deposited my checks but had never really looked at them closely enough to know that I was getting the flex dollars. They told me the next open enrollment time was not until January 1990 and that I could sign up for insurance then.

I decided I would wait until January to go to the doctor. "It's not a big deal, since I never get sick," I thought to myself, forgetting all about the lump. Since it had been so long since my last one, I did make another appointment for the Pap smear and decided to pay cash for that.

I went to my appointment with a new doctor that a friend had recommended. After he completed the exam, as he was walking out the door, I suddenly remembered the lump.

"Doctor, I forgot to tell you that I did a breast examination a while ago, and I thought I had a lump. Can you please just check it for me?"

"Sure. No problem," he said, as he walked back into the room.

I lay back down on the table, lifted my shirt and bra to expose my breast, and pointed almost right to the spot.

"Yes, I feel it too," he said, as he examined my right breast.

Then he examined the left breast.

"I don't feel it on the other side. That means it is unilateral. I would like to see you again in about two weeks to see if it is still there. I know you are paying cash for this, so I won't charge for the second visit. Just call my nurse, and you can come in. I will just check it for you and make my recommendations. I would probably tell you to get a mammogram, just to be sure. Okay. See you in two weeks."

He looked at the nurse and said,

"Have her make an appointment on her way out."

This was a little more disturbing to me because I thought, "Why does he want to see me again?" This was more difficult to ignore than me finding the lump had been.

Chapter 9

Beach therapy

Two weeks passed quickly, and the doctor told me this time that I should get a mammogram. Now I had a problem, but I was still only thinking of the money and of the fact that mammograms cost money. My plan was to wait for two and a half more months, until I had insurance, and then get the mammogram. I still didn't believe I had any chance of having cancer. I started to wonder what I would do if they did find something. It would be pre-existing; would my insurance even pay for it? It was strange to be thinking about something like cancer because I felt perfectly healthy.

A few weeks passed. I did worry-mostly about money. My friend Leslie was tired of teaching school. She needed a break, so over the weekend, we decided to take another trip to California. Leslie was a friend whom I had met on my mission, but I had never had a chance to really get to know her until I went to a mission reunion in that same month where we were able to talk more.

The night of the Mission reunion, where I met Leslie, I was feeling like I did not want to go probably because so many of them were now married, and it reminded me I was not married. I told myself that I would go and would make one new friend that night. I am so glad I set that goal because that is the night Leslie and I became good friends and finally had the chance to really get to know each other better.

Shortly after that mission reunion, Leslie and I were off for some fun at the beach. It was already late October. This was just a quick four-day weekend "simply because I missed the ocean" type of trip.

As soon as we arrived, we went straight to the beach. Again I started thinking about Adam—probably because in the past I had spent quite a bit of time at the beach with him. I looked up, and again, there he was! I had even gone to a different beach than before, so I really did not expect to see him there. He was walking on the boardwalk, and we both saw each other at about the same time. We walked up to each other, but I kept my distance.

He said, "I was just thinking about you, missing you, and here you are. This is strange. Did you move back?"

I answered his question: "No, I just drove in from Utah and came straight here."

He said, "Are you sure you didn't move back and you're just not telling me?"

I told him I had not moved back. "I don't lie, like some people I know," I added.

Leslie quickly came to my defense.

"Yes, she lives in Utah, and so do I. So she is not lying to you."

She knew who he was because I had confided in her about him. Leslie then went for a walk on the beach and left us alone.

This time I used the opportunity to say all of the things I wish I had said the last time I saw him. I had an opportunity to purge myself of this guy once and for all—to get all of my anger out and confront him with all of his lies. I watched him try to hide his humiliation at being caught, revealed completely in all his past lies to me. This was my second chance, the one chance a woman usually does not get. It took less than an hour to tell him everything I wanted to say. When I was done, I started walking toward Leslie. He grabbed me and kissed me again. I walked away mad at him, but he didn't seem to care. I felt sorry for the woman he would someday marry. He was fun, but it would have been hell to be married to someone like him. I had fun telling him off—for me and all the women he had done wrong and would do wrong to in the future.

After the experience at the beach, we went straight to the Santos's home. Their home always felt like a second home to me. When I was young, Joe and Helen Santos watched my four sisters, my two brothers, and me, whenever my parents were out of town. They were like grandparents to us because they would take us on day outings to places like Disneyland and Knott's Berry Farm. I remember once when we were little, they had loaded all of us into their Volkswagen bug and took us to Universal Studios. Sometimes we would spend the night at their house. They would make us hot fudge sundaes and let us stay up late watching movies on TV. We would sleep on the fold-out bed on the couch. It was always a time of special attention when we stayed at the Santos's home.

Now, whenever I brought a friend to their home when I was passing through, they always made time for us and welcomed us with a good meal and a place to sleep. Sometimes they even took us out to eat.

I remember when I was in the fifth grade Helen Santos took me shopping and bought me at least three very nice outfits with hats, tights, matching shoes, and a nice winter coat. They had also taken me with them on vacation to Utah once to visit some mutual friends of theirs and my parents. My parents later met up with us in Nevada at our family's ranch.

Mr. and Mrs. Santos, or Brother and Sister Santos, as we called them at church, only had one son who was married and out of the house since I had remembered spending time with them, and now the Santos son was married and had five children. Brother and Sister Santos spent much time with their five grandchildren. About eight years before, when I was twenty-something and teaching swimming, they had me teach two of their grandchildren.

Jessie, one of their grandsons was now staying at their home for the week. He remembered that I had taught him to swim, but I had not seen him since then. He looked very grown-up-like a man. He spent a lot of time talking to Leslie and me, and it felt as if he was flirting with me.

As we left the next morning for Mexico, I told Leslie that "I think he was flirting with me." I told Leslie how his grandmother Sister Santos told me at breakfast that he had paid me some compliments that morning to her. He had said to his grandmother, "She looks as good in the morning as she did at night." I was flattered. However, I know how I needed to watch out for these younger guys that possibly were just seeing me as a challenge for an opportunity to date an older woman.

Leslie and I had another fun trip to Mexico and spent the night with our friend, Carol Harvey Stewart, in San Diego. This time Carol did not go with us to Rosarito because she was quite sick from a pregnancy with her first daughter, Shanise. She had been teaching aerobics at the time, and she was so skinny because she could not keep any food down. I was worried about her health, but we enjoyed her company for a few hours before we had to leave. It was always very fun to see her.

The next day, we came back to the Santos's house. Jessie was still there, and his grandparents took us all out to dinner. Leslie and I had planned to go to a church dance. Jessie had also decided to go, and several of his friends were going with him. They planned to follow us in Leslie's car to the dance.

That night at the dance, Jessie kept asking me to dance all night. I was flattered again, and there really wasn't anyone else to dance with. Besides, he was a really good dancer and his friend was asking Leslie to dance all night too. Leslie and I just laughed to ourselves about these younger men we were dancing with. Actually, we were having a really fun time too.

Jessie asked me to dance a slow song-the last song of the night. When it was over, he kissed me on the cheek. I backed away. It really took me by surprise. I walked away from him. He followed me and apologized.

"I'm sorry I kissed you," he said. "But I really enjoyed dancing with you tonight."

He and his friends invited us to go out for something to eat. As the night progressed, although I found myself entertained by his charm and wit, I planned to keep my distance. I sat about three feet away from him as we talked.

While we were talking alone, I noticed Jessie was staring at me. Then he said something I did not hear, so I said, "What?"

He said it again. "You didn't give me a star in the backstroke."

Right then I remembered him as a little boy, standing in front of me on the last day of swimming lessons, and I was explaining to him that he had stars on everything but the backstroke because it still needed a little bit of work. I remembered telling him,

"Look at all those stars you got. You did really well! You're a great swimmer!"

Back then I knew that he was not pleased that he did not get his star for the backstroke.
Then he said,

"I thought you were so cool, and then you crushed me by not giving me a star on the backstroke. Then I told myself that you were not so cool, after all. Yes, I had a crush on you when you were my swimming teacher."

I was flattered again by his sweet confession.

The weekend flew by, and it was soon time to go home. On the way home I found myself thinking of him and how charming he had been. Before I had left, he had asked me if he could write me, and he wrote down my address. He had also asked if he could give me a hug goodbye, so I let him.

During the next two weeks, he wrote me twice. His letters were also fun and charming, and I enjoyed the attention. I told him we could be friends. He wrote about his plans to go to college and to go on a mission. I thought since I had already experienced that part of my life, I might be a good friend to him. After all, I enjoyed his friendship. So, I wrote back to him and encouraged the letters. I really did enjoy his company and all of his kind, charming words. And yes, I was a little physically attracted to him, even if I wouldn't admit it to myself. It felt safe to flirt a little-after all, he was in California, and I was in Utah.

Upon returning to Utah, I became busy with my work at the Children's Hospital Residential Treatment Center (commonly known as the R.T.C.).

Chapter 10

Enjoying my job as a Recreational Therapist.

As a Recreational Therapist, I scheduled recreational activities and directed the after-school hours of 24 latency-age emotionally disturbed children. The activities I planned aimed to promote healing from abuse and to help the children reach age-appropriate developmental milestones.

In addition to these responsibilities, each staff member was assigned a child with whom he or she would do fun rewarding activities with, like movies, shopping for a toy, and the child could make behavioral contracts with the staff for additional rewards. These activities were planned to help provide extra motivation for the children regarding their treatment and to work on their target behaviors.

I had been assigned to work with Sarah, who was six years old when I first met her. Never before had I met a child like her. She was a survivor, a fighter, and an eternal optimist—against all odds. She had been born into a horrendous abusive situation and had come out of it at age five into the foster care system. She was lucky enough to stay in a foster home that was one of the best in the state. She had an inner strength that had helped her to get what she wanted, a family. She knew she had started out life in a terrible environment, yet it seemed that a belief instilled in her from above told her she deserved better and that she would someday, in the near future, have a loving family. She told me,

"I believe I will have a mom and a dad and at least one sister and brother."

This dream lived strong within her heart. I believe it was the only thing that helped her through this difficult time in her life.

Sarah and I had a special relationship from the very start. I enjoyed her company, and she enjoyed mine. At night, before she went to bed, she sometimes asked me to sing the "Lead Me, Guide Me" song. I didn't know what she meant until one day at church the congregation was singing I am a Child of God:

> I am child of God
> And he has sent me here.
> Has given me an earthly home
> With parents kind and dear.
> Lead me, guide me. Walk beside me
> Help me find the way.

> Teach me all that I must do,
> To live with Him someday.

The next time I worked with her and every time after that, I always sang the "Lead Me, Guide Me" song to Sarah before bed.

One day, we went shopping at a children's clothing store in Park City. Sarah tried on dresses and modeled them for me. I am sure she was hoping I would buy them for her. As she tried on these elegant and expensive dresses, I felt her strong self belief that she would someday have the best in life. She wore those $80 to $100 dresses like a little princess. Unfortunately, she left that day with only a small pair of dainty, lacy socks. I later went back and bought the dress. It was given to her for her birthday from the hospital.

When I spent time with Sarah, I felt as if I was spending time with my best friend. I felt so many rewards for the little bit of time I gave her. We were kindred spirits, laughing at the same things, loving the same feminine styles of clothing in the stores, and dreaming of far-away places that we hoped to see together someday. One day while we were driving in my car to go out for an ice-cream cone, she looked up at me and said, in a dreamy, six-year-old voice: "Nancy, maybe someday we can go to the beach together." I had not mentioned how much I loved the beach. She caught my attention. I, too, wished I could someday show her the beach for the first time. At times I wished I could adopt her. I thought about it often.

At times, Sarah got angry because her dream of getting a family was not happening quickly enough. Her therapist tried to explain that these things take time and that a judge made all the decisions—that we could not make things go any faster for her. She decided to write a letter to the judge. In the letter she told him that she wanted a family for Christmas this year—in one and a half months. There had to be a mom and a dad and at least one brother and sister in that family. Her letter was direct and demanding; after all, she was angry. We helped her mail the letter and explained to her that it probably would not happen that fast. She insisted that it would.

Soon after she wrote the letter, a family visited another boy at our facility. When they met Sarah, she crawled up on the mother's lap. She knew this was her new mom. They began home visits, and by Christmas, much to everyone's surprise, this strong-willed little girl had her family. They decided to adopt the boy and her. She went to live with them, and the adoption began its course toward finalization. I missed her, of course, and I was very happy when her family invited me to be her "Aunt Nancy" and to visit her whenever I could or wanted to.

Meanwhile, while I was enjoying my time with Sarah, I was trying to figure out what I should do about the lump but I was still busy with other important things. Because I was single and didn't have children of my own, I loved everybody's children. I also spent a lot of time with my nieces and nephews who lived close by.

There was also another significant younger person in my life at the time. In 1988, I had met a fourteen-year-old Chinese boy named Matt. Since I had served a mission in Hong Kong and spoke Cantonese fluently, we became good friends. He was a troubled teenager in a California hospital's adolescent unit where I was the Recreational Therapist. I also met his mother, who didn't speak good English so we communicated in Chinese. Matt was later sent to a long-term treatment center in Utah—shortly after I had moved to Park City. I had visited him one time while he was in Utah because his mother had put me on his approved visitors list.

Unfortunately, before he was ready to go home the insurance ran out, he was discharged and sent home to live with his mother and stepfather in Southern California. Soon he was back with the same crowd of friends and getting back into drugs.

Later, now at age 15, he was a runaway living on the streets in Provo, and he called me. Since he had run away in the summer of 1989, we had been in touch several times while he lived on the streets. I was meeting him on the BYU campus approximately once a week.

The first time, we contacted his parents. His parents were tired of all his lies, and they did not want to rescue him from another problem. They also felt that he was fairly safe on the streets of Provo, compared with his neighborhood in Santa Ana.

Another time, we met for a meal of Chinese food and to talk. I liked Matt from the very beginning when we met at the hospital in California. Even with all of his self-imposed problems, he still had an element of sincerity to him. However, it was difficult to see through all of the fast-talking manipulations back then. Inspite of this, we became friends. Now, in Provo, again our paths had met up. He was trying to establish himself to live in Utah and go to school, to stay away from the negative influences back home in California.

As we met each time to discuss his plans, he was always appreciative and kind. He would speak frankly and openly about life. He seemed to know that there was something better for him too, much like Sarah did. He also seemed to have been humbled by living on the streets. He had been making changes—nothing drastic—but small changes were occurring. I know that prayer had become a part of his life. I would imagine that being alone on the streets there were times when it became easy to depend on God and to speak to Him. Or at least, it seemed that way to me as Matt spoke of his hopes and how he was praying and working for them to come true.

Again, because I was single, I had time to help him. It felt good to be a listening friend. I was careful not to enable him in his problems. Mostly, I just listened. I believe the most I ever gave him was a nice Chinese dinner and a Mexican blanket. I believe his parents were wise not to rescue him when he chose to run away to Provo. I would imagine they would say they made this choice out of desperation, not inspiration, since they had been dealing with his problems for already about two and a half years.

I remember several significant times when we would meet. One time we met in the Student Wilkinson's Center at BYU. I asked what he wanted to do, and he said bowling would be fun so we went bowling. Another time, I asked him if he was hungry, and he said he was so, I took him to a favorite Chinese place down the road toward Springville. He told me how much he missed his mom's cooking. After our food was served, He asked me,

"Aren't we going to say a prayer on our food?"

I replied,

"I do not usually pray in restaurants or public places but if you want to we can. How about you say it?"

"Okay I will." He replied.

He bowed his head and said a humble prayer. His prayer was the same style of praying that just 3 years ago as a missionary I had taught others how to pray. First, you address your Father in Heaven usually something like, "Dear

Heavenly Father." Then, you thank him for blessings in your life. Then you ask him for blessings or special needs and last, you close in the name of Jesus Christ, Amen.

> I looked at him and I asked, "Where did you learn to pray like that?"

> He looked down at the ground and said, "The missionaries taught me."

> "When did they teach you? Did you get baptized?" I asked.

> "No. My parents would not let me." He said still looking down.

> "I think you'd better start praying to get yourself off the streets." I told him.

Another time after we met it was getting colder, and I gave him my Mexican blanket from my car. He looked different this time. I asked him how he was doing, and he said,

> "Something happened to me. I have been praying."

He said, "One day, around noon, I was walking by the Marriot center, and I saw all these people walking out. I then noticed some of them were Chinese students, and they were like glowing. I want to be like them (I thought to myself). I told myself that this is what my mom wants me to be like."

He then told me,

"I called some staff people from the treatment center I was in to see if they could help me."

He continued to tell me all about his prayers being answered. He eventually ended up talking with Mr. Williams, his previous therapist in Provo. They were all trying to find a place for him to stay and go to school. I could see that he was changing, and it was exciting to be a part of it. I felt like a missionary, but I missed my Hong Kong friend Carol Harvey being with me. It brought back old memories helping Chinese young men embrace gospel principles. I was excited to tell Carol about Matt.

As you can see, my life was full. I was busy with a full-time job and with spending time with sweet Sarah and with my friend Matt. I was also working for the National Ability

Center (then called Park City Handicapped Sports Association) as a swim coach for the Special Olympics, and I was substituting in the Park City school district and for the LDS high school seminary program. In addition, I was taking a religion class at the University of Utah Institute of Religion (a training class for people who are interested in teaching LDS seminary full time) and was also spending time with my family-not to mention having a social life with my friends in Park City. I believed that life was supposed to be full of meaningful, rich experiences. If there was a way to make it all fun, that was even better. I really didn't have much time to think about the lump.

Although in the back of my mind I remembered the lump and did think about it, I just kept putting off going to the doctor. I strongly believed that there was no way I could have cancer—I was just too young and too healthy!

Chapter 11

Pretending to be someone else.

In my journal, I can say anything, and I think that is why I always enjoyed writing in my journal. Sometimes it was the only thing that kept my head on straight. One day, on my day off, I was sitting in my house in Park City writing in my journal. I decided that I should just pay cash and get the mammogram and stop worrying about it. Then I would finally know there wasn't anything wrong. The doctor had told me it cost only about $50 or $60 for a mammogram.

Still, I knew that if the doctors found something, it would be a pre-existing condition, and my insurance would not pay for it. I really wanted to wait, just in case they wanted to remove the lump and conduct a biopsy. I knew that it would cost me thousands even for just the removal of the lump. Then I thought to myself, I can go to a mobile mammogram, pay cash, and use a fake name. They would give me the results right there, and I would know that there was nothing to worry about. If they did find something wrong, I could go ahead with the treatment and figure out later how to pay for it—or I hoped that my insurance might pay for it. Actually, it was Carol, my sister, who had suggested I use a fake name. She has always had a talent for making things happen. Besides being a hard worker, I suppose that is why she wins all of those sales awards and makes such good money in her sales position.

My roommate Jeri and I spoke during breakfast, and I told her I was thinking of using a fake name to get this worrisome thing behind me. Jeri offered me her name. I could pretend I was her for the day, she said. Since she didn't mind and I had her permission, impersonating her did not seem like a bad idea.

So, I called around to find a mobile unit, but I couldn't find one. Therefore, I went to the only major hospital that was not part of my soon-to-be health care plan. I was happy to see that it had a state-of-the-art women's center with brand-new equipment. It felt strange to check in with the receptionist using Jeri's name. The form asked for my birth date and social security number. "Darn, I don't have it," I thought. I slipped over to a pay phone, hoping someone would be at our house and could help me find out Jeri's information. Jeri answered. I whispered into the phone; "Jeri, good you're home. I need your social security number and your birth date." Jeri laughed and gave me the information. I completed the form using her name, her social security number, but used my birth date. I just felt like I wanted to have something of mine when I checked in.

The nurse came in and told me to undress from the waist up. She gave me the top half of a disposable hospital gown and told me to put it on with the opening in the front. All the time she was giving me directions, she kept calling me Jeri. She explained what a mammogram was and what she would be doing to take the pictures. Then a second nurse came in to help her. She seemed to be the head nurse and was doing some training of the other nurse. She introduced herself as Nancy. I could not help but smile.

They began talking amongst themselves as they positioned me up against the machine, squishing my breast between the two flat surfaces. They kept telling me to let them know if it hurt too much, calling me Jeri the whole time. As the younger nurse continued her training, she would say, "Nancy, can you check this angle?" Several times I almost responded when she said Nancy, and sometimes I would forget to respond when they called me Jeri. It was getting very confusing!

They took many pictures, positioning me in many different angles. I was amazed that they actually expected me to allow them to squash my breast between those two cold, flat panels over and over again. Any other x-ray I had undergone in my life had been a breeze. But this was really painful, and they kept saying, "If this is too painful, let me know."

Just when I thought they wouldn't inflict any more pain, I watched them pushing the remote again, squishing my breast even flatter. I endured it for the sake of my life, all along thinking to myself, "Who invented this machine? It must have been a man because a woman would have known how painful this is."

After it was finally over, Nurse Nancy said, "Please wait here, and we will see if we have some clear pictures. Don't get dressed yet, because if it isn't, we will have to do it all over again." Needless to say, I prayed for a good picture. The thought of having to endure that again was not my idea of fun.

The head nurse came back and told me I could get dressed. She said she wanted to talk to me after I was dressed. I dressed quickly, and within moments, she was knocking at the door. She escorted me into a small office and told me to have a seat. Nurse Nancy's face was showing signs of distress.

Her first words to me as she began to speak were, "Jeri, I understand that you do not have any insurance—that you are paying cash for this today." She proceeded to tell me that my mammogram was showing micro-calcifications on my lump, that this didn't necessarily mean cancer was present, but that a needle biopsy would need to be done to determine whether or not the lump was cancer.

I listened, giving her my full attention. She kept calling me Jeri.

"Jeri," she said, "this is probably not cancer. But if it is, you don't have any insurance. I understand that you will have insurance at the first of the year. Now, if this is cancer—and I am not saying it is—but if it is cancer, let's face it. If it is pre-existing you don't have the money to pay for it, and your insurance does."

This woman must have seen the horror in my eyes as she told me I might have cancer, and she was still calling me Jeri.

I then looked at her and said,

"So what you are telling me is to pretend that I never came here today to avoid a pre-existing condition."

My newfound friend who shared my same name, Nancy, said to me,

"Jeri, I hate to be so unethical, but let's face it. You don't have the money to pay for this, and your insurance company does."

I looked at her and said,

"As long as you are being unethical, let me tell you this. I am not really Jeri; but my name is also Nancy. It is Nancy Gibson. I was afraid of this happening, so I decided to use a fake name because I really hoped I would find out there was nothing wrong with me at all."

Her face changed from sadness and distress to shock and relief. Her mouth literally dropped open.

Then she told me,

"I know a surgeon who is just starting out, and I believe if I asked him, he would do the needle biopsy for you and post-date it so your insurance company would pay for it."

She was actively trying to help me save my life—if it was cancer. She had never laid eyes on me before that day, but she was trying to save my life and financial stability by nonetheless lying and seeing that I got the necessary treatment in a timely manner. She was attempting to carry me through this difficult moment in my life, and she was willing to help at all costs. I had just met her, and in my eyes she was an earthly guardian angel in my time of crisis.

I told her I didn't know what to do—that I would need to go home and talk to my parents. I told her I had a brother-in-law who was a doctor who had previously done his internship at a facility within my same healthcare company. I thought he would know more about how the insurance company would deal with my predicament. I thanked her for everything and told her I would get back with her. Needless to say, I left the women's center in shock, especially since I didn't believe I had breast-cancer in the first place.

Chapter 12

Resolving the insurance problem.

I drove straight to my parents' home and told them. We then called my brother-in-law. He told me that I should appeal to the insurance company through Human Resources, since it was their fault, in a way, that I didn't have insurance. It was my lack of responsibility for not noticing that they were giving me flex dollars, but it was their fault for having me work on the day I was supposed to complete the paperwork in the hospital-wide orientation. I then decided it would be better to go the honest route. I would have to go get another mammogram—this time with my real name, and with my Health Insurance provider.

I called back my friend Nancy at the Women's Care Center and told her about my plans. I told her I was just going to hope and pray the insurance would pay for it, and that it would all work out somehow. Since I had forgotten to pay her, I asked what I owed her for the mammogram. I told her I could bring the money over right then and asked her to tell me exactly how much it was.

She replied, "Honey, you don't owe me a thing. I have your file in my locker, and I wiped your name off the computer. All you owe me is a phone call at the first of the year telling me how you are doing." I thanked her and promised I would call.

My brother-in-law told me to the hospital to get another mammogram. He also gave me the name of a surgeon to call for the needle biopsy. I was able to get in for a mammogram that week. That night I went home and wrote the following in my journal:

Dear Journal,   December 8, 1989

Today I went to get a mammogram because I have a lump in my right breast. I'm scared. They said I will have to have a biopsy because it looks suspicious. It may not be anything but a cyst or a benign tumor. I guess I just don't know how to deal with this because I have never really experienced any real illness in my life. I have always been really healthy, so I feel very confused and scared. I have to say my honest feelings at this point are that I am not really scared to die, but I'm very scared to lose a breast. The thought is really awful.

I am young, single, and it doesn't seem fair. I am probably overreacting to this, but I am worried. And then there is stress of not having insurance because my insurance isn't good until January 1990. So I've got to wait another three weeks until the biopsy. Before that, I need to get another mammogram so it isn't pre-existing on my insurance. What a nightmare. I wish I just knew what to expect. The nurse today was very nice. So needless to say, this day I am grateful for the simple things right now, and I am trying to not worry about everything in my life.

Last night was the last class for my Institute class for teaching seminary. I have been thinking of trying to get hired as a full-time seminary teacher, so I will be a student teacher this coming semester. It should be fun for 5 weeks. I do wish they would hire me, but who knows? Anyway, life isn't bad. I was going to say it's good, but it doesn't seem that way today.

> Thanks for Journals,
>
> Love,
>
> Nancy

Chapter 13

Getting a second mammogram.

There I was, undressing again from the waist up and going through the same process with very little emotion this time, since I already knew what they were going to say. I decided I could not wait 3 more weeks and I would just have to fight to get my insurance back dated. Now this time I was me, and the nurse was just another friendly face. It all seemed like a blur in the race against time.

Within a few days, I had met my surgeon, who performed the needle biopsy (with no insurance yet). The needle biopsy was a quick process, and it was a good thing because it hurt like hell. They told me it was a good sign if it was painful when they stuck the needle in the lump. Sometimes when a lump is cancerous, there is no pain. They stick the needle directly into the lump and attempt to draw fluid. Apparently, if they can draw fluid, it is supposed to be another good sign- which they also were able to do.

I left that day feeling much more hopeful that the lump wasn't cancer—particularly when my surgeon, told me there was only a 10-percent chance that it was cancerous. As scared as I felt, I gladly hung on to any hope that was offered to me. That night, I went home and wrote the following.

Dear Journal,   Monday, Dec.18, 1989

Hi! Well, so far I've had the second mammogram, with the same results. I went for the needle biopsy. Tomorrow I'll find out if it is positive or negative. I will need to have it removed no matter what because the needle biopsy isn't 100 percent accurate. But the best news is that last Friday, when I went to the surgeon for the needle biopsy, he said there is only a 10 percent chance it is cancerous. I was feeling much better with this news. Not so scared, anyway.

Yesterday, Sunday, I decided to fast. My mom told me she had called the Santos family and told them about my problem, and Sister Santos (Helen) said she and Joe would fast and pray for me. When my mom told me this, I started to cry to think that they would do that for me. Sister Santos also told my mom that they were going to a church party that night, and they would tell the other Church members to also fast and pray for me. I really felt like crying that anyone could be so kind and loving as Joe and Helen Santos. They always made me feel so important and loved.

Yesterday, when I decided to fast, I went to church, and Sister Francis in my ward gave a very spiritual lesson in Sunday school on "The Pure Love of Christ." It was a beautiful lesson. She asked the question, "Who in your life you would like to tell that you love them and you haven't?" I immediately thought of my dad and mom, so I told myself today when I go to my dad and mom's house to get a priesthood blessing, some way I will tell them I love them.

That day, my dad gave me a beautiful priesthood blessing. In the blessing, he said that the problem would be resolved, and he blessed the doctors that they would do a good job and have the wisdom to know what is best for me. He also blessed me that I would be able to serve others who are less fortunate than I am. I loved this blessing, and afterwards, I hugged my dad and I whispered in his ear, "I love you." It seemed as if he was happy that I said it. Oh, yes—in the blessing, he also said or blessed me that I would know how much he loved me. From the words of the blessing: "you will know how much we love you."

Later that night, my dad and mom invited me to go to their stake Christmas fireside. Elder Marvin J. Ashton was speaking. He spoke on what Christmas is. I love to hear him because he always makes everything so simple and clear. He was talking about the importance of family, Christmas, and the Savior. As he spoke, I felt a great love for him, and I cried. My favorite thing he said was that the most important thing that happened to him that day was when his four-year-old granddaughter said to him before sitting down to dinner, "Grandpa, can I sit next to you?" This took me by surprise because I thought he would say something more magnificent because he is a great leader in the church. For example, he might have said the most important thing that had happened to him that day was taking the sacrament or even meeting with the prophet, but he didn't. He talked about the simple words of a four-year-old who knew she loves her grandpa. This is why I love Marvin J. Ashton so much. He truly is a people person—someone who loves people deeply. I admire him. I guess his message to me was, "If you have done it unto the least of these my brethren, ye have done it unto me."

My mom saw me crying when he was speaking, and she whispered to my sister, Missy, who was sitting next to me, "Put your arm around her." So Missy told me, "Mom says I have to put my arm around you," as she pulled me close.

After the meeting, my mom hugged me, and I whispered in her ear, "I love you." Then we both cried harder. I don't think I was crying because I was scared—I think I just felt the Spirit that night. Then, as I was quickly leaving the fireside because I had to go to work, my mom hugged me again, and I said, "Don't worry. It's really no big deal." I don't think that comforted her very much because she looked scared for me.

I don't think there will be any problem, but if there is, I feel stronger—like I can somehow get through this because of all of the support and love I have from all of them. I love Christmas time, and I am thankful for journals where I can say anything!

Merry Christmas!

        Love,

        Nancy

Chapter 14

Meeting with the doctor.

On Monday morning, I went to work and left early to go to my mom's house to call the doctor for the results of the needle biopsy. The nurse told me the results would not be available until Tuesday, the following day. I felt relieved that at least it was not bad news. I decided not to worry yet and to just go on with my day. Besides, I could tell that my mother was worrying already-enough for the whole family of nine plus all my friends put together.

Tuesday came quickly as I kept busy and then called the doctor. His words were kind, sympathetic, warm, but scary. He said, "The cells look highly suspicious, and we need to talk to you in the office today."

My mom and I went down to his office within the hour, still not knowing if I had any insurance. He was very supportive and kind as he told me I had cancer. In fact, I don't recall he even said I had cancer in those exact words. He simply presented my treatment options almost as precautionary procedures but with a clear message that these were the only options I had.

He said, "Your choices for treatment are to have a mastectomy or a lumpectomy with chemotherapy. The two approaches are equally effective in all of the studies that have been done, so it is really your choice." He continued on to say that a biopsy and a lumpectomy would need to be done quickly. He told me that he would like to do the procedure that Thursday morning—just two days later.

Just as he said this, his nurse called him to answer a phone call in his office. As he walked out of the room, I looked at my mom, who was looking rather shocked.

I said, "I cannot have a mastectomy. That just isn't fun." Then I thought, "What did I just say?" Then I laughed at myself and said to my mom, "Did you hear what I said? I said that I can't have a mastectomy because it isn't fun—as if I expect everything in life to be fun." As I continued to laugh at myself, I was grateful to have the other option where I could keep my breast. I kept looking at my mom, who seemed to be looking at me as if to say, "How can she be thinking like that?"

As I sat waiting for the doctor to return, I thought to myself, "What if I do have to have a mastectomy?" I remembered the Ann Jillian story I had seen. "Could I get through an experience like that?" I was only 32 years old and I had never been married. "What is fair in all of this?" I wondered. I somehow really did not get the memo that life was not fair and that sometimes it certainly wasn't fun. Suddenly, I realized that the whole experience—cancer—was a big deal. But I also hoped I could get rid of it, maybe? These were my thoughts as I sat quietly with my mom.

The doctor came back in the room, and I told him my choice to not have a mastectomy—not even knowing all of the effects chemotherapy would have on my body. The idea of losing my breast was not even an option for me. I then told him about my insurance problem. He told me he would schedule the surgery for Thursday morning, on an outpatient basis, and that his nurse would give me a paper that explained the time I needed to be there and the instructions before the surgery. He explained that he would take out the lump and some of the tissue around it, as well as the lymph nodes to be tested to determine whether the cancer was spreading. He then said he would call the Benefit's Director in the Human Resources office and would tell them they needed to take care of the problem immediately because he didn't want me worrying about insurance coverage while I was going into surgery.

We went into his office and phoned Human Resources. I listened in. I heard him say, "What do you mean you haven't made a decision yet? Can't you call a special meeting with committee members? If not, then there must be someone who can make an administrative decision in your department. I don't want my patient having any additional stress from worrying about this while going into surgery. It's not healthy for her to worry about whether this is going to be paid for or not when it is your fault she doesn't have insurance."

He was great. He spoke with so much authority. I felt supported. They must have been telling him the same things they had told me earlier—that it was the Christmas season and people were already leaving for the holidays, so the written appeal I had sent would not even be looked at until January when the committee met again; the matter was impossible to settle now.

I heard my doctor say, "I think you can do something, and you need to. Goodbye." He hung up the phone and said, "I think they will take care of it now," with a smile on his face.

"He's good," I thought to myself. "That's the kind of man I want operating on me."

My mom and I left the office. She went home, and I had to go into work and let my supervisor and colleagues know what was happening.

I went in to work, and I told my boss, Tim, the director of the Residential Treatment Center, that I would be having surgery. He told me he would also call the Benefit's Director and put pressure on them from his side.

I took care of some preparations for the annual Christmas party that we, my coworker and I, had planned for the children. I saw a friend, Ned, one of the therapists, an LCSW (Licensed Clinical Social Worker), and I told him about my surgery. We were sitting downstairs, near my office, talking about how I was going to get through this. I told him that I had said, "I can't have a mastectomy. That just isn't fun."

"Those were the first words out of my mouth," I said. I then explained to him how all of my life, I had expected everything to be fun, and if it wasn't, I tried to make it fun, or I didn't do it.

He looked at me and said, "Well, Nance, I guess you will have to make this fun." His words told me that my philosophy was not trivial, nor shallow—that it was okay to be someone who enjoyed making life fun. I will always remember that moment as a turning point in my life because of his sensitivity to my need to have things be less serious. I took that challenge seriously, and it became almost a motto or theme for my fight for life.

From that point, I tried to deal with cancer the same way I dealt with any other mundane, common, everyday task. I would take care of business and try to have fun doing it. Especially when I began to feel scared, I tried to focus on the good and fun in all that I did. I was not going to let having cancer stop me from anything that I wanted to do. In fact, I tried to do just the opposite. I vowed to do all of the things that I had not done in the past—for whatever childish reason. I would now do my best at them, in spite of the situation. I refused to let this setback affect me negatively.

In some ways, this motto became my diversion from reality, but it also became my strength. It gave me a way to deal with things. I became so busy that I barely had time to worry about anything. Between having fun going for treatments and work, I would be staying very busy for the next six months.

I finished my preparations for the Christmas party. Everything was ready except for decorating the gym; we would do that the next day. I left early that day, unable to concentrate, and went home to my house in Park City. I wrote in my journal:

Dear Journal,

Today I found out that the needle biopsy shows very suspicious cells, and I will need to undergo an immediate partial removal of the breast or a mastectomy. I decided to go with the partial removal-a lumpectomy with chemotherapy—because I just don't want to have my breast removed unless it is absolutely necessary. I can't imagine losing my breast. I mean I just cannot do that. It would be too hard for me. I think about it, and I feel like my life would be incomplete without all of my body. I know that the doctor would give me another breast but I heard if they do they still use your nipple and there is always a chance that there could be a cancer cell in your nipple and then you could go through it all over again. Or they can give you a breast without a nipple but that would look weird. I have never been married, and I fear that my husband will not be happy with me if I had a missing body part.

My surgeon is a very nice man. He was very supportive and helpful with my insurance problem. Life is scary and very sad, but I am trying to make it not so bad. Today I laughed at myself because all of my life I have always expected everything to be fun and if something isn't fun, then I just don't want to do it. So somehow I hope this experience will be at least meaningful, if not fun. Oh, well, I guess it really isn't going to be fun! But it will be meaningful because already I see how much people love and support me. I have many friends and loved ones who care a lot. I am very fortunate! That's all for now,

        Love,

        Nancy

Chapter 15

Trying to make surgery fun.

With a positive attitude to mask my fears, I prepared to put up the best fight ever to be fought. I attempted to refocus my thoughts by thinking about the Christmas party the next day rather than the surgery.

The next evening, the Christmas party was a success. Sarah received her pink ballet slippers in her stocking, thanks to the Monument Park Ward who prepared a beautiful stocking filled with wishes-come-true for each child. Family members, staff, the children, and members of the church group all experienced a beautiful spirit of Christmas giving. There was a musical program, and much love abounding, but when it was all over, there was nothing left but surgery the following morning. It seemed to just hit me like I had run into a brick wall and there was nowhere to hide from my cancer diagnosis anymore. That night after the party, I walked out the door at work, my thoughts were: I have cancer.

While I was driving home, these were my thoughts: "Tomorrow they will cut me open, and it might be bad." I began to cry and plead with God. As I was driving to my mom's house, I recalled my thoughts from the day before when I was feeling scared, when I had prayed and I had been given a comforting inspirational thought given to me from above by the Great Comforter. "If it gets too bad, there are always miracles." I began to cry so hard, and I almost hit the van in front of me. I looked up and I saw a BYU bumper sticker on the van. Next to that BYU sticker was another sticker that read *Anticipate Miracles*!

I cried even harder, but this time it was tears of joy because I knew I did have help from above. Not only did I have support from my family and friends, but I knew that miracles could happen and that miracles had already happened. Once again, I felt that God was watching over me.

That night, my father gave me another blessing. He blessed me that the doctors would be successful with their efforts. I was spending the night at my parents' house because I had to be at the hospital at 6:00 a.m. Before bed, I showered, blow-dried my hair with some curl, and then I painted my toenails. I knew I would not be feeling that good after surgery. I tried to make myself look my best so I might feel better and in case anyone came to visit me. I went to bed late that night, and I got up early. I couldn't sleep, but I did look good.

In the morning my mom and Missy, my younger sister, came with me to the hospital. I was very anxious. Keeping with my motto, always have fun, I was still trying to make this whole experience fun.

When we arrived at the hospital room, I was told to undress and put on the hospital gown. I was trying to see the humor in just about anything I could, though at the same time I was running the risk of looking as if I had lost my mind. As I wore my drab hospital gown, I was thinking how much easier it would be if I could wear something a little more colorful or festive. Maybe a nice Hawaiian print could cheer things up! I began to say these kinds of things out loud to my mom and my sister.

I looked around the room and noticed how sterile and technical all of the medical apparatus in the room looked and how it all screamed "Surgery." I said to my mom and sister, "You would think those who designed this room would know that people in hospitals don't need to be reminded what they are here for. They are quite aware. Why not help them forget? I would design this room to be much more people-friendly. Perhaps each room could have a theme. You know, if my hospital gown is Hawaiian, why not a Hawaiian tropic room?"

"Nancy, are you feeling okay?' Missy said, in a sarcastic tone. My mom just looked at me and shook her head.

"If I were hired to design this room," I continued, "I would do it to help people feel better. I would think of comfort and serenity. I would try to camouflage some of the equipment and would put some glamorous, comfy furniture in here. It needs to be non-threatening—or at least not so scary looking.

My mom and sister were looking at me as if I were crazy; and then the nurse walked in to start the IV. She took my arm, poking me ever so gently, and then told me she was going to start an IV and that an orderly would be in soon to take me to surgery.

In a friendly, kind voice, she asked if I had any questions. I said, "Not really." in a flippant tone of voice.

She left the room, and once more, I began complaining.

"I cannot believe it is 1989 and we still have not come up with a better method than using an IV. Why do they have to hook you up like this? You would think that someone would have invented a nice time-release capsule that you could swallow with flavors, like chocolate ice-cream or lobster and butter. Or, it could have multiple flavors like a gourmet, six-course, time-release meal that you could be enjoying while you're having the surgery. Or, if you don't like the time-release capsules, then they could at least have something pleasantly chewable.

"Picture this: the nurse comes in on roller skates and whips out a menu, asking you what flavor of IV you prefer. Now that would both relax and distract me. I wouldn't even know I was in a hospital or about to have surgery. Sounds like fun to me! You would think they could wear something less like the traditional hospital garb. Their attire needs work, and so does this hospital gown!"

My rambling efforts to relax myself seemed to be working temporarily. I did not feel much like someone who has cancer or who was about to have her breast cut open.

The orderly came into the room. He was a tall, 20-something guy with a kind of bounce in his step. He seemed cheerful and upbeat. His brown hair and kind of attractive looks with his good eye contact was very refreshing. His carefree attitude seemed to say he had nothing to hide and took me by surprise. He came toward me pushing a gurney up to my bedside and said, while raising his eyebrows at me, "Want a ride?"

I pleaded with him, "Please, let me walk. I don't need a gurney." To me the gurney was just another reminder that I was about to have surgery. I told him, "Really, I can walk. See, look at me. There is nothing wrong with me. It is after surgery that I will need that."

"It is hospital policy-you have to ride," he insisted with a smile. I thought of Jessie, the Santos's grandson, and how Helen Santos had told me about how he was an orderly in a hospital too, and how he truly cared for his patients and would often use his sense of humor to put them at ease. I then climbed aboard, and he began strapping me in.

I cheerfully waved good bye to my mom and Missy as he began to wheel me down the hall. As I lay there, I suddenly realized that I had to go to the bathroom and started thinking what would happen if someone was under anesthesia and had to go to the bathroom. I visualized the doctor performing surgery as he suddenly sees urine dripping off the operating table into a puddle on and around his scrub shoe covers. As I began to worry about this, I quietly said to the orderly,

"I have to go to the bathroom really bad."

He replied in a cheerful voice,

"That is okay. We will just take a detour."

He began pushing me away from the operating room and I remember several nurses asking him,

"Where are you going with her? They were yelling out-loud, "You're going the wrong way."

He announced in a very loud voice to all of those concerned,

"I know, but she has to go to the bathroom."

At about that time, I was covering my face in embarrassment. He unstrapped me and my IV. I pulled my IV along and ventured into the bathroom.

Afterwards, he strapped me back onto the gurney. Once more, he began pushing me to the operating room. This time the trip seemed to go quickly. I found myself pushed to the side by the wall, right outside the door of the operating room. There was now a nurse at my side that explained to me that I needed to sign some papers to allow the anesthesiologist to start general anesthesia process. She then announced that the first shot would take effect rather quickly and that the second shot would be given right before the surgery.

As she gave me the first shot, it wasn't the anesthesia that I remember feeling. Instead, at that moment, I felt fear and the reality of what was happening. All the reality of having cancer, which I had been trying to minimize, hit me at that moment. My emotions broke lose like a dam in an earthquake. However, on the exterior, my tears gently flowed out like the droplets from Weeping Rock at Zion's National Park.

The nurse noticed the tears gently running down my face and said to the other white-jacketed bystanders, "She's scared" (as she tried to calm me by rubbing my lower leg). She then introduced me to my anesthesiologist. He told me I would begin to feel very relaxed. My surgeon was there too. He spoke to me in such a kind voice and looked very serious as he explained the procedure that was about to take place.

I felt another surge of emotions, and the tears seeped out a little harder this time. Time seemed to slow to a crawl. It felt as if even my tears were coming out in slow motion too. I was then wheeled into the operating room, and several white-jacketed staff carefully lifted me from the gurney onto the operating table. They then quickly turned their backs to face the supplies on the counter top and appeared to be preparing for the surgery.

I lay there in the middle of the room, and then suddenly I realized,

"This isn't fun. I'm scared."

Desperately and impulsively in my semi-sedated state, I blurted out,

"Does anyone in here know any good jokes? Because I really feel like I need to laugh."

The people in white coats and scrubs turned around and looked at me, with surprise on their faces. Then a blurred face with a kind voice came closer and said,

"Now let me see—I heard one the other day. It goes like this: What did the duck say to the cashier at the store when he wanted to buy some Chap Stick?"

I responded, "I don't know. What?"

"Just put it on my bill."

"Ha, ha! Thanks," I said in a tired voice.

"You see I have this philosophy of life, which is: Life is supposed to be fun. No matter what the circumstances are, life was meant to be fun." I told him it was my goal to try to make this fun, so that was why I wanted to hear a joke."

He replied, "That is a good philosophy. I think I will adopt it for myself."

From right about then on, I can't remember a thing. I was out.

When I began to come to awareness again, I was in the hospital room with my mom and sister. I remember a lot of discomfort and feeling pain. It wasn't until the nurse came in and asked if I needed some pain medication, which she then gave me that I began to liven up. Then my mom told me I had some visitors while I had been under the anesthesia.

My co-worker, Lisa, had come with some flowers and a card with many signatures from my friends at work. My sister's father-in-law had also come by to give me support. He had recently gone through triple bypass heart surgery. He had struggled in the last few years with heart problems and yet was an inspiration to me because he still enjoyed skiing and horseback riding as well as other physical activities.

I lay there, trying to ignore the pain and trying to go back to sleep with the hope to reawaken with less pain. Time passed quickly as I slept most of the day away.

I left the hospital that evening, and I went to my mom's home. I can't remember much except that I had a drainage tube attached to the area of surgery to drain the excess body fluids. I was told it would be with me for a week or so. Christmas was five days away, and I would not see the doctors until after the holidays.

I arrived at my parent's home, and I went to sleep in the bedroom next to theirs.

Chapter 16

Recovery

Over the next few days, I received visitors, cards, flowers, and money, as well as a new journal from my oldest sister Carla, for me to write about my experiences. She also wrote me a letter to tell me about her Bell's palsy diagnosis that she had gone through. She said the experience had taught her to appreciate the little things and the most important things in life. In the letter, she told me to use my cancer experience in the same way. Carla was more than a big sister sometimes; she was like a mother to me too. I admired her.

With all the visitors and support, I thought to myself, "I have so many dear family members and friends. I am the luckiest girl in the world." In the next few days, I was visited by many friends, bringing flowers and cards. Monica and Amy came and brought me a red rose. Shelly, one of my roommates, came and brought my mail. Laura Lee, a roommate from college, came and cheered me up with her fun personality. I always loved talking with her because she is refreshingly honest. I felt so lucky to have friends who took time out for me this close to Christmas when everyone was so busy. "I am the luckiest girl in the world—or am I?" I wondered to myself.

Two days before Christmas—still at my mom's house, I lay in bed feeling very unsure of my future. Then, the phone rang. It was my doctor. My mom brought the phone to me. I was surprised because I didn't expect to get any results of the biopsy until at least a few days after Christmas.

He said, "Hi. I have a Christmas present for you."

"Yes," I said rather anxiously.

"The lymph nodes we removed were all negative for cancer!" he exclaimed with a cheerful tone.

"Thank you for calling and telling me this," I gratefully responded.

"You just have a Merry Christmas, and I will see you later when we get the pathology reports back," he said.

To hear this news, I suddenly felt as if my life had been given back to me. This meant that the cancer had most likely not spread anywhere else. I knew there were still many more treatments ahead of me, but I felt so grateful to have this good news and that my doctor had taken the time to find out the results of the biopsy on the day before Christmas Eve and to call me personally to give me the good news. This helped to make my family's Christmas a better one.

The next day, on Christmas Eve, I got up in the morning and wrote in my journal:

Dear Journal,   December 24, 1989

It's Christmas Eve, and yesterday I received the best Christmas present of all—no cancer in my tested lymph nodes! I received the call on Christmas Eve morning and he said, "I have a Christmas present for you. The tests of the lymph nodes came back, and all of the 25 nodes were negative."

Before we left in the morning for my surgery, my dad and mom had a family prayer. After the prayer, I told my Dad that I loved him, and he said back to me, "I love you." That is twice now in one week. This is really getting easier now!

After my surgery, I had a bag to drain the surgery fluid from my body. It bugged me a lot, but I was just glad that the surgery was over. The ice felt good on it, and the pain pills really helped, too. I love all my friends and family who visited me, with cards, flowers, and get-well wishes. I feel loved!

Later that night, the day after the surgery, I started to get really scared that maybe the cancer had spread and I'd have to have chemotherapy for a long time and maybe eventually lose my breast too. I started to feel depressed, and I was crying. My Mom came in and saw me crying. I said, "This is harder than I thought it would be."

I have been on a roller coast ride with my feelings. I have faith that I won't die, but I seem to not have faith that I could lose my breast and maybe have to go through this more than once. These are my thoughts sometimes. Then someone seems to come along each time I am down and take my mind off of my worries.

The next day, I received flowers from my friends in California: Carol, Jill, and Debbie. It is a really cute Christmas arrangement. I got more flowers from my roommates, Shelly, Karen and Jeri, including a little Christmas present. Shelly also brought my mail. There was a letter from Jessie Santos. He's so sweet. He didn't mention the surgery so I don't know if he knew about it. I also received a new diary and $50 for new shoes from my oldest sister Carla (she knows I need them). She also sent me a very supportive letter. Everyone called a lot, too. Then when the doctor called I was so happy I don't even remember what I said to him. Probably "Thank you," and "Merry Christmas." We started calling everyone to tell them the good news.

That was so nice of him to call me. He was leaving for vacation, and I wasn't expecting to hear from him until Wednesday after Christmas. It was so kind of him to take his time to call me before his vacation to let me know the results.

Well, today is Christmas Eve. I feel very blessed and in debt to my Heavenly Father that He was there for me and answered my prayers. I am so happy to be alive and loved. I want to live and love always. I am thankful for all my friends and family members that are there to help me through this.

That's all for now.

Love, Nancy

Chapter 17

Radiation & chemotherapy

Christmas came and went. Some of the family lived far away and were not able to come to visit us that year. We had fun with all those who could get together on Christmas Day. My sister Carol was expecting a baby girl any day. Carol lived in Draper, only about ten miles away. We were all anticipating another miracle, the miracle of bringing a baby into this world. How wonderful to have this joy of birth in our family! I thought. I recorded another entry in my journal on December 28:

Dear Journal,   December 28, 1989

Well, life is good. I've just been lazy lately, hanging around with everyone at my mom and dad's house. I went to the doctor yesterday, and he didn't have the pathology reports back yet, so he couldn't give me any additional information yet. I will find out more when he gets the reports. The pathologists are probably still celebrating the holidays. I will be going to see my doctor again on the second of January—next Tuesday. He is such a nice man. Everyone has been such a support to me—my family, my co-workers, and my friends, with flowers and cards. The Santos Family also sent me a card and it had $50 in it. I am spoiled.

Today I got paid at work, so I am paying my bills. It is always nice to have money to pay your bills. Plus it looks as if I will be covered by the insurance after all. It looks promising, and I have been fighting for it, so hopefully things will work out there, too. Everything is going great since I heard the good news that the cancer has not spread into my lymph nodes—which means it probably has not spread into any other parts of my body. Yeah! But I still have moments of fear, but I am fighting it.

I did find out that I will need to get six weeks of radiation, five times per week, Monday through Friday, plus the chemotherapy. I will know more about it next week.

This week my little six-year-old niece, Ella, has been here at my parents' house. She has been so sweet. She tells me she loves me several times each day and gives me lots of hugs and kisses. She is so sweet and fun. When she heard I was going to have chemotherapy and that my hair would probably fall out, she told me, "Your hair is so pretty," as she stroked it tenderly. "Can I have it when it falls out?"

My sister, Carol (Ella's mom), said she thinks the baby will come today. We still don't know for sure if it is a boy or a girl yet. It will be fun, either way, to have a new baby around the house. I will love holding it. I hope that I can have babies someday when I meet the right guy. I do know that many women have had babies after breast cancer treatments so I think I will be able to. I always wanted 10 children growing up, but as I get older it has changed to however many I get will be just fine. So anyway, life is good, and I'm basically happy!

Thanks for Journals,

Love, Nancy

I was feeling better, and I was getting out a little. I went to a movie one night, and I was no longer spending all of my time in bed. My doctor would not allow me to go back to work for three weeks, so I was just taking it easy.

I was also thinking of buying a plane ticket to California with my $50 from the Santos's and $50 from Carla. (The shoes could wait.) I was also thinking about how nice it would be to spend some time at the beach since I couldn't work anyway. I was starting to get bored. I had to do something besides read.

Then I found myself thinking of Adam and remembering how he used to make me feel loved whenever I would leave his house, and he would always say, "Be careful." I wondered about what he would do if he knew I had cancer, and I missed the fun we had had together. It was not an option for me to call him. Besides, I didn't think it would even be that easy to reach him by phone. He wasn't a real prospect for the lasting kind of love I dreamed of having someday, yet I believe that he did love me in his own way, as much as he was capable of loving someone. He never said anything bad about me to my knowledge, but maybe he did to all those other women he was also seeing when he was saying "I love you" to me. He never said anything bad about me even when I told him off and said how angry I was and what I thought of him.

I told myself that I was just lonely, wanting male companionship, and that it was only natural for me to think of the last man I had felt love for. I quickly rationalized away my thoughts of him.

On December 30, 1989, I wrote:

Dear Journal,

    Tonight I feel very emotional, and I miss Adam very much. I miss him because I'm still in love with him and feel the hurt from the lies he told me, but I also remember the love I felt from him, even though I feel very cynical sometimes when I think about him. I guess I really loved him a lot. Or, am I just lonely and scared, and he was fun, so it is normal to feel this way? I did have lots of good times with him that I didn't write about in here. He was so gentle and kind sometimes. Yeah, I must just be lonely. I went to a movie tonight, and it was a love story. It looked so good to have someone to love and love you back. The movie was called *Always* with Richard Dreyfuss and Holly Hunter.

    Sometimes I hate having to have this surgery. It still hurts a lot. I want someone to love me and baby me, I guess I want Adam. I wish he had made me hate him the last two times I saw him. The last two times I was in California (September and October), I just ran into him on the beach, and we talked for a long time. Even when I was telling him off he was still kind to me. He said to me, "I know it will never work for you and me because I blew it, but it hurts me because I love you." Of course, I couldn't believe him or trust him. I was afraid of believing him. Oh, well, life is good, and this depression will pass. I just wish I could see and talk to him right now to get me through tonight. I need him, but it is dumb because the truth is, if he cared, he would have called and gotten in touch with me or come to visit me sometime. I guess it's a no-win situation. Anyway, I have been so bored lately. I need to ski.

I tried to go to the temple today, but all of the temples were closed. Missy and I first went to the Jordan River Temple, and it was closed. Then we went to the Provo Temple, and it was closed. I guess they are all closed for the holidays. I just need to get back to my life.

Today I started watching a PBS show that had been videotaped about Poetry, the Power of the Word, a Bill Moyers special. It is about four hours long. It has been really interesting and uplifting. I think I will be able to use this video in my work when I do poetry workshops with the patients.

There is a poem about Magic Johnson on the tape. When you hear it the language makes you feel as if you are watching a basketball game. I might even get some teenage sports-minded boy to like poetry with that poem.

There are many interesting and beautiful poems on the tape. It reminds me of the day I was at the beach reading a poetry book, and Adam told me that his favorite poem was "Secret of the Sea" by Longfellow. I love that poem, and it was as if he could just look inside of me and say the right things to make me love him. I don't know--maybe I should call him. I do still love him. I'm just afraid of being hurt. I'm going to pray to see if I should call him or not. That's that. I need to know. The funny thing is I do know I should never call him because he can't be trusted so I won't but I want to. Why do I want to call him? Because I think I need to be loved and with him at times I did feel loved.

Love, Nancy

Chapter 18

Promises of adventure and marriage

Still without any news of the pathology reports, I decided to go to California and have some fun since I didn't have to go back to work for another two weeks or more.

I flew into LAX in Los Angeles, and Joe and Helen Santos picked me up. I planned to stay a week—a week to spend time at the beach resting and swimming in the ocean in December. (I have always gone swimming in December.) I was lucky because it was pretty good weather that week. I walked out to the water and went straight into the water. It was cold as the water splashed against me, but it felt soothing to me. The smell of the salty air and warmth of the sand between my toes were calming to me. The cold water felt good on my scar. I had heard that salt water is healing. As I swam in the ocean, I felt healed. At the beach, cancer had absolutely no effect on me. I felt as if I could do anything; my traumatized, stiff, swollen, nerve-damaged arm felt fine out there in the refreshing cold Pacific Ocean.

As I enjoyed swimming in the ocean my thoughts went back to being 12 years old and swimming out to past the breakers all alone. Swimming in the ocean felt as comfortable to me as sitting in an overstuffed easy chair watching Saturday morning cartoons. The ocean had always been my friend. Once more, the ocean knew exactly what to do to make me feel great.

With the unusually warm weather for January, I even got a little bit of a tan—just a healthy-looking glow.

Later at the Santos's house, Joe and Helen were taking took good care of me, as always. I had been in California and had enjoyed two days, and I did not feel that I wanted to call Adam.

The last two days had been relaxing. I had enjoyed talking to all of my Long Beach friends without it being long distance. Many of these friends I had gone to school with me and I had known most of my life.

I asked Helen what Jessie had been up to and why he had not been over yet. She said, "I didn't know if you wanted to see him, so he doesn't know you are here. All we need to do is to call him, and he will be here." So she did. She told him, "There is someone here who wants to speak to you," and then she handed the phone to me. We talked a little, and then he came over, and we talked a lot. I told him about my cancer. It was interesting to talk to him because he had taken care of many cancer patients in his work at the hospital as an orderly.

He asked me what I was planning on doing and how long I would be there. I told him I was there to relax at the beach and to visit friends. He told me he could take a few days off, and he could drive me around wherever I wanted to go. I told him that my friends could come get me, but he insisted that he would do this and that it was not a problem. He ended up taking most the week off and drove me all over Southern California visiting my friends.

I returned home, and those times of worry were still pending, with pathology reports still unknown. So far, I had experienced mammograms (two of them) needle biopsies, and a lumpectomy with removal of the lymph nodes. Still to come were radiation treatments and chemotherapy.

I didn't find out the results of the pathology reports until I went to the Salt Lake Clinic to see an oncologist for my chemotherapy. My oncologist explained why I would need chemotherapy even though the results from my lymph nodes were all negative. He told me that my pathology reports clearly showed that my cells were cancerous. The good news was that we had caught the cancer early. It was in Stage I, and the lump was 1.5 centimeters-about the size of a small peanut. He also explained that the cancer cells were estrogen-receptor positive, which meant that they feed off the estrogen in my body. He also explained that the cancer cells were aneuploidy and that means that the DNA in the cells is radically different than that of a normal cell. He explained that this meant the cells had become strong and were capable of metastasizing. Particularly because I was young (my cells were more active than those of an older woman), I was at risk for a reoccurrence. He also gave me a choice. He said, "If you don't choose to have this treatment, there will be a 30-percent chance of reoccurrence. With the treatment, there will be only a 1-percent chance of reoccurrence." I had expected all of this. I found it interesting to hear all the facts and felt comforted by my doctor's ability to explain things so clearly to me.

    I started the treatments in a few days, still thinking a lot about everything that had happened in California. I wrote in my journal the following:

Dear Journal,   January 12, 1990

I have a lot to tell you about what happened in California, but I am very tired and will write later because I need to rest tonight. Today I started chemotherapy, and it kind of makes me feel sick, so I am going to rest. If I wasn't feeling so tired, I would write and tell you how it all happened, but I will rest for a while and then write. California always seems to be my escape from whatever.

January 13, 1990

I wanted to tell/write about what happened when I was in California. Originally, I went to California to go to the beach, see my friends, and get away from all the medical stuff that has been happening. I hoped I would see Jessie Santos because I had thought about him and all his flirtatious fun letters he wrote to me. I enjoyed all of his attention and the way he treated me. I was also a little afraid he might be like Adam and that I was just a challenge to him. Possibly he just wanted to see if he could "get the older woman." We had about 13 years between us. I had not really thought of having a dating relationship with him because of his age. My ego was fragile, and I did not want to be hurt by a younger man, so I told myself I would enjoy his company and compliments and that would be it. When he did come over to see me, it was great to talk with him, particularly because of his experience working with cancer patients at the hospital as an orderly.

I had planned to go to a church dance while I was there, and my friend Hope was going with me. Hope and I had been good friends since high school. Jessie took the night off from work and he also went to the dance. He went with two girlfriends. I didn't know if one of them was his girlfriend or not; I was there to just have fun.

Then something happened. Something I did not plan. We were all standing there at the dance, listening to the music and talking, when suddenly Jessie was gone and disappeared into the crowd. I looked through the crowd to see if I could see him. He was kneeling next to a girl who had collapsed on the floor. He looked as if he was checking her pulse and checking for breathing. He looked as if he was positioning her for emergency first aid. He stayed with her until the paramedics came and took over. I watched him take care of this girl, and suddenly all of my pride and my fear of what others might say left me and were replaced with an admiration for his compassion for the girl and his instinctive abilities of being able to take care of her medical emergency. I suddenly lost myself and thought of him. I was thinking how great he had just handled that situation. I observed him in a selfless act of service and caring for someone he did not even know.

He then walked back to me, and he didn't say a word, but handed me his watch and walked out into the hallway. I asked his friend where he was going, and she said to the bathroom to wash his hands. So I followed him into the hallway, and I waited outside the bathroom. When he came out, I walked up to him, handed him his watch, and gave him a big hug.

He looked at me as if he liked it and said, "What was that for?"

I said, "Just because."

He gave me a look that seemed to be saying he liked me, and I gave him the same look back. He looked away and seemed scared and stressed from the emergency situation he had just dealt with. I told him I was impressed with the way he had handled the situation. I was complimenting him, and then he was complimenting me back. He then asked me to walk with him down the hallway, and I did. As we walked, we were walking closer and closer to each other. Then, as we got down to the end of the long hallway, we kissed. It felt right.

He asked me, "Do you want to go somewhere and talk?"

I said, "Yes." He ran and got the keys to his friend's jeep and said, "Come on. Let's go somewhere."

We drove to a fast food place and got something to drink. Then we sat in the jeep and talked.

We talked about the age difference and he said, "You're a person, and I'm a person, and we like each other. Age doesn't matter."

I felt that he was right, but I worried about it more than he did. I shouldn't have, but I did. I spent a lot of time with him, and I can tell that his grandparents knew we liked each other. One time when he was dropping me off at my friend's house before he left, he gave me a hug, and I started to say, "I love . . ." but then I stopped.

He said, "What were you going to say?"

I said to him, "I don't know. It just seemed natural to say that."

He said, "Well, I love you, too. Good night."

I really do feel like I love him, and I feel very happy when I am with him. I know that age is a factor, and that he is in a huge decision-making time in his life. He is deciding whether or not to go on a mission and what his career will be. I have been through all of this. I hope I can encourage him to go on a mission because I know from having been on a mission how valuable it can be to teach you what you need to know. It teaches you things that can help you be successful in life.

I do feel kind of strange letting myself like him, but we are both adults, and we are just being a support for each other. It has only been a week, and, I really do miss him and all of the fun we had together. Anyone would love him.

I also wanted to write that today that my doctor gave me permission to go ski with some international cancer survivors at the Park City Handicapped Sports Association. It was great to be on skis again and very rewarding to be able to ski with them. I skied with Alma from Mexico. She is 22 years old, and she had her leg amputated 10 years ago from cancer. She also had one year of chemotherapy, and it was good to talk with her. I was impressed with her ability to live her life to the fullest and to be out skiing with only one leg, but I know people like her don't focus on the fact that they only have one leg. Instead, they just live life and enjoy it.

Three days ago, when I talked to my chemotherapy doctor for the first time, I found out that I will be getting six months of treatment. I was scared to hear this news, but I thought of Jessie, and his compassion gave me strength. He's pretty wonderful. I really love him.

Thanks for listening.

Love, Nancy

I had started chemotherapy, and it made me very sick. I was taking CMF, which is a combination of three drugs. Cyclophosphamide (a colourless fluid) also called Cytoxan is given as an infusion or by tablet. I was taking it daily in pink tablets. Methotrexate (a yellow fluid) is given as an injection along with an infusion of salt water (saline) into your cannula. 5FU (a colourless fluid) is given as an injection in the same way. The simple explanation is I was taking CMF. The C is for Cytoxcin, which I was taking orally and daily. The M is for Methotrexate, which as given to me intravenously every Friday. The F is for 5FU. I would have treatments for two weeks, and then I would have two weeks off, although I would still take the Cytoxin daily during those two weeks. This course of treatment would last for about six months.

On January 21 1990 I wrote the following.

Dear Journal,

Today at church I was given a new calling. I am the new Blazer A teacher in primary. I love teaching these sweet little boys. Before the Bishop's counselor called me to this position he said he had prayed for me because of my illness. He told me that when he was praying, three things came to his mind regarding me. He told me that he didn't know why he should know these things, but he felt he should share them with me. He told me, "First he knew that the cancer would not come back and that I would live a long and healthy life." I have also had this feeling; actually it's knowledge probably because of my patriarchal blessing.

Then second he told me, "You have no idea the things that are in store for you in your life—great things, adventurous things that would make you very drained at times. The Lord will bless you that you will accomplish much in your life." This too I have known from my patriarchal blessing but not to the degree he talked about.

Lastly he said, "There would come a time in my life when things would slow down and I would wonder why the Lord didn't have anything for me to do. It would be a space in your life and at that time a man would come into your life and you will get married." Basically he said I had a lot to look forward to in my life.

I prayed about this when I went home, and I feel like it's true. So I guess I better keep working toward my goals. I am excited about life. I have tons to look forward to. Anyways that is enough for now. I'll write more at a later time.

Love, Nancy

Chapter 19

Loss of appetite

I was back working full time again. I felt good about myself, and I was ready to take on the chemotherapy and the radiation. I went to LDS Hospital to meet with the radiologist. He told me what to expect. He said that I would come for treatments every day, Monday through Friday. The treatments themselves would only take about two minutes, but I should allow myself time to change clothes and for the technician to position me on the table. He also said they would be able to position me rather quickly, in the exact spot, because of the tattoos they would be giving me. That was the first I had heard of any tattoos. He explained that they would be the size of a small freckle and that if I wanted them taken off at the end of the treatments, they could remove them for me. He also said that some of the side-effects of the radiation treatments were severe sunburn and nausea, as well as some firming of the tissue. I thought, "Firmer, tan breasts?" I can live with that, but the nausea, some of which had already experienced with the chemotherapy, did not sound fun.

Next, I was lying on an examination table with two young guys who were radiology technicians. They walked over and opened my hospital gown in front, revealing my breasts. I felt like this can't be good with two guys looking at my breasts. They were moving them and marking on them. They were drawing lines on my breasts. I was trying to act natural but it felt very strange to me. Then one of the guys stopped what he was doing, looked at me and said, "Now, did you say you wanted the eagle tattoo or the rose?"

He caught me off-guard and then I smiled and said, "Both sound nice either one." They continued drawing all over me, using tiny measuring instruments to prepare the exact spot for radiation. They joked with me as they pretended to be drawing an eagle and a rose all the time they worked. I was grateful for their sense of humor to help me feel more comfortable.

Every day I would go back for treatment, I would start to recognize the other patients. Most of them were older than me, and many were older than my parents. There was one woman who was closer to my age. We would talk a little bit, even though there was not much time. She was from Idaho. They would call my name, and I would go in and be out and heading back to work within five minutes. Some of the people who were waiting were inpatients and looked very sick. When I saw the other patients, I always felt sorry for them and extremely grateful to have the problems I had.

I was handling the Cytoxin fairly well and only had mild nausea from taking it. It was the injections and the drip every other Friday that I couldn't handle. The first time I received a treatment, I went back to work but then left after a while because I had thrown up and felt weak. The doctor gave me some Compazine for nausea, but I felt that it made the nausea even worse, so I never took it. We tried another drug, too, but it didn't work, either. The next time he tried giving me the steroid Dexamethasone with the injection and the drip. It worked. This was the only thing that allowed me to function on the days I received the Methotrexate and the 5FU.

I had pretty much lost my appetite; I had to make myself eat. In the mornings, the only thing that sounded good was individual packages of instant flavored Quaker oatmeal. I would mix the oatmeal with water and put it in the microwave oven for about 40 seconds, then eat it without any milk.

One day when I was feeling pretty good, a friend took me to lunch at Ruth's Diner up Emigration Canyon. I ordered a spinach salad, a favorite of mine. It was a relaxing lunch, and later that day, I went for my chemotherapy drip and injection. On my way back to work, I had to pull the car over on the side of the road and throw up. It took me a long time to like spinach salad again. Needless to say, I didn't have much interest in food in the next six months.

Chapter 20

Work & losing my hair

Work was going very well. Sarah was with her new family and was doing very well. I was assigned to a new child—a little boy from a neighboring state named Sean. Sarah had been at the facility the first day he came. They were sitting at the lunch table together, and Sarah whispered to me. "I have a crush on the new boy." He was a skinny little toe head with black rimmed glasses he was wearing because of his lazy eye. I enjoyed my time with him. He was on a special program because he had failure-to-thrive syndrome (a condition caused by lack of love, when a child stops growing and developing and becomes very malnourished). Sean's special program was to ask anyone he wanted to hug him whenever he thought he needed it. Even though he was six years old, you could cradle his small frame in your arms and rock him in the rocking chair quite easily. He was smart and manipulative, and whenever he was in trouble, he would look at you and say, "I think I need hugging time."

"After you finish your consequences," I would say. I spent quite a bit of time holding Sean and rocking him, and I bonded with him.

Outside of work, I had also been visiting with Matt, my Chinese friend, from Santa Ana, California who had been living on the streets in Provo, Utah. He had made some incredible changes while now living with a family that had taken him in under a strict behavior contract. He had been getting good grades and working. He felt he was almost ready to go home to California to live with his parents. He had also become interested in the Mormon faith and was taking the missionary lessons as well as taking a Book of Mormon class through his high school seminary program. He was learning about life after death, and since he knew that I had cancer, he would sometimes ask me about life after death and if I was afraid to die. He wanted to know the answers and began to study about the plan of salvation. He had prayed and read the Book of Mormon, and he had recently decided to be baptized. He said at first he prayed about the Book of Mormon, but he could not get an answer. He kept praying and one day he asked God, "Why can't I feel anything about the Book of Mormon when the

Missionaries have promised me that I would know of the truthfulness of it if I prayed?" He said an impression came into his mind very clearly. The words that came into his mind were, "You will not get an answer until you are truthful with the Williams family." He had been allowed to live with Alene and Dan Williams under a strict contract, and although he had broken the contract, they did not know. Shortly after moving in with them while he was working at a local restaurant as a dishwasher, a co-worker had asked him if he wanted to get high. Matt decided to go with his friend and get high. It was something he was used to doing for most of his teen years. The spirit impressions clearly told him to tell them the truth. Matt was very scared to tell them because he was sure they would kick him out of the house. He had grown to love this family and did not want to lose them in his life.

He finally got up the courage to tell them, and to his surprise, they were impressed with his truthfulness; he was allowed to stay. He prayed again to know the truthfulness of the Book of Mormon. The answer came quickly this time. He now knew it was God's word.

Matt invited me to give a talk at his baptismal service. I felt honored that he asked me. His parents came from California to see him get baptized and to take him home. I was amazed to see the change in this young man—as were his parents.

After he was baptized, there were several of his friends that had also been with him in the same treatment center in attendance. I saw Matt walk up to one of them named Andrew and ask, "So Andrew, did you feel something good at my baptism today?" Andrew humbly responded, "Yes I did." Matt, a natural born missionary, continued on to tell him "That feeling you're feeling—it's the Holy Ghost bearing witness of the truthfulness of this gospel." Matt would become an important and significant friend in my life. Andrew was baptized too not long after in Santa Monica, California in his hometown.

While going through my treatments, I had been thinking a lot about death—not so much for myself, but for others. I would see other patients at the hospital while I was receiving my radiation treatments. It was hard to see people who were obviously suffering and then not to see them anymore, knowing that they were losing the battle or wondering when

I didn't see them any more if they had lost the battle. It was particularly hard for me to see my younger friend from Idaho, who had lost all of her hair. Even though we didn't speak much because we were in and out of there so quickly, I felt saddened, and I wondered if she would make it. I thought of the many mothers who would leave behind children as they passed on to the next world. I sometimes felt guilty because I knew I wasn't going to die and that others would. I had no children or a husband to leave behind. "Why not just take me?" I sometimes thought to myself.

Somehow, though I knew I would not die because of inspiration from my own prayers being answered and the revelations given to me through priesthood blessings, I knew that my life was not over and that someday I would be married to the right man and would also have children. I believed there was one man for me because of some personal spiritual experiences I had in my life. I didn't know who he was or where to find him, but I knew that I would someday meet him. Meanwhile, I would wonder about each new man in my life that I felt love for and would ask myself the question, "Is he the right man?"

As the chemotherapy treatments progressed, I kept watching for hair loss. At first, I could not notice any. I would watch to see if there was a lot of hair in the drain at the end of each shower. Then, a few weeks after the second IV treatment, I did begin to notice an increase of hair loss, and it became progressively worse. I was reluctant to comb my hair because it fell out so easily. I also started wearing it pulled back in a ponytail to the side (a hair style influence from the 80's) because it was easier than brushing it and running the risk of losing a chunk of hair.

The phone calls and letters from Jessie were a comfort. I was not dating anyone, although I had always had lots of friends, male and female, to do things with. I was still hanging on to the support I was getting from Jessie, by talking on the phone, but I was also busy, so our relationship was not a priority.

I had told the mother of a friend of mine about Jessie, and she told me about a woman she had known who didn't get married until she was 36 years old. She worked in the BYU University Library where she met a man 14 years younger. She ended up marrying him, and they were very happy. When I heard this, I felt better about loving Jessie. He was definitely someone special to me. I did not know what role he would play in my future, if any at all.

I particularly appreciated my friends in Park City: Karen, Marian, Amy, Jeannie, Tracey, and Kevin. One Friday evening when I was feeling sick from the chemotherapy, Karen came over and brought me 7-Up, soda crackers, and a magazine. She and all my friends were kind to me and a huge support.

The people at my Park City Ward at the church I attended also called and checked up on me. I was attending church every Sunday and was fortunate enough to teach the 10-year-old boys in Primary. They were very fun. There were three of them: Aaron, Stevie, and James. Aaron, I already knew because I had been his swimming teacher for the last two summers when I taught in the Park City Handicapped Swim Program. He was a sweet young man with special needs and he had "pretend friends" who would come to Sunday school class with him. He was mentally challenged—I think he had some form of Autism. His pretend friends were named Shark and Jesus, and we would set up chairs for them in class because they regularly attended Sunday school with Aaron. He also liked to bring his long rubber snake to church with him. Frequently, he would speak to his snake in the middle of the lesson or have conversations with Jesus, too. I really enjoyed working with those boys. I was so impressed with how Stevie and James accepted Aaron's differences and frequently helped me get him back in his seat. Having this responsibility to teach them was truly a blessing in my life. I also enjoyed singing the Primary songs—particularly the "Lead Me, Guide Me" song, in Primary each Sunday, and I would think of little Sarah.

Life was moving fast. One day Jessie called me and told me he wanted to come to Utah to visit me. I was so happy to just hear his voice. He still had not made any decisions about his life. Since my hair was falling out, I was worrying about what I would do if I lost all of it and was completely bald. After we had been talking for a while, I told him that my hair was falling out and that I didn't know if I would have any hair when he came.

His response was so natural. He candidly said, "Nancy, who cares if you lose your hair—you still have two breasts."

I laughed out loud and thought to myself, "He is good for me, and I hope I'm good for him. I do love him as a friend, but I think I'm falling in real love with him. I think about him all the time."

More and more I kept thinking, "This is hard losing my hair, I mean, it is really hard." Lately, I was finding myself looking at women's hair and wishing that mine was thick again. I felt depressed. Every day was a permanent, bad hair day.

Everything else in my life was good, though, and I felt positive about my treatments. I was doing my own guided imagery in the car on my way to work. I would listen to relaxing music and tell myself I was free from cancer. For my guided imagery, I would visualize water running through my body and through my veins, washing it clean from cancer. The visualization of the water washing through every part of my body in my mind was a healing image. Water was always soothing to me, and so it made for a perfect healing image. I was trying to lead my mind and body to a better place—a place of healing. I was happy to be alive, and I wanted to stay that way.

But sometimes I still found myself feeling sorry for myself because my hair was falling out. I would then feel guilty because I felt this way, and I would tell myself, "You should be grateful-you are alive." I especially felt terrible for having these thoughts when I would see another person who looked very sick coming in to get chemotherapy. Then one night, I was watching the news, and the newscaster said, "Women who are going through chemotherapy said the worst part of this treatment is the hair loss." When the newscaster said this, I felt so comforted to know that I wasn't bad or vain to miss my hair and that most women going through this same experience felt the same way I did. I felt validated and quickly forgave myself.

Finally after six weeks, I was almost finished with the radiation treatments, and I really felt that I was lucky because it really didn't seem to have many side effects for me. I was receiving the chemo and the radiation the same time so it was hard to know which treatment was causing which side effect. It seemed to me that the chemotherapy caused all of the problems for me. I had lost my periods completely; the doctors had told me that this would happen. They said sometimes they come back, and sometimes they don't. I believed that mine would come back since I had a strong belief that I would have children someday.

My life had settled into a routine of treatments, work, and many other activities. I was also student teaching an early morning seminary class at Highland High Seminary at 6:30 a.m. every morning. Sometimes I would stay at my parents' because it was easier to get there on time than when I stayed at my house. I enjoyed the contact with the high school students. I really like working with adolescents. But I had been so busy that I was not writing in my journal much. Finally, on February 17, 1990, I wrote the following entry:

Dear Journal,   February 10, 1990

I started writing this on the 10th but didn't get too far, so now it is the 17th of February. This last week has been a difficult week. I missed Jessie. I didn't get any mail or even a phone call for a while now. I realized how much I relied on him for support. Needless to say, I cried a lot this week. On Valentine's Day, I was getting my radiation treatments, and the nice tech said,

"And how has your Valentine's Day been?"

I started to cry. He said,

"What's the matter?"

I didn't want to say anything, but he was so kind and persistent that I finally blurted out,

"I didn't get a valentine from my friend in California."

I couldn't believe I was crying like that! Then I thought that it must be my hormones, especially since I wasn't having periods like I should be.

I finally decided to call Jessie since last time we had talked (on the 10th) everything had seemed fine, and he was planning to visit sometime in the next month or two. When I called him, he couldn't talk because he was washing the dog. He said for me to call him back in 10 minutes, and I did, but the number was busy for a while. (He lived with his parents and two brothers and two sisters, so this was not unusual.) Then I called back later and got his answering machine. I thought maybe he just was outside for a second, and I tried again. It was busy for another hour! I started thinking about what he had told me his mom had said when he had told her about us. She said, "Jessie, you'd better not hurt her." I started to believe he was going to hurt me. I guess I could survive, but I would really miss him a lot. I love him. It feels like love, anyway. I need him. It just seems too hard. I wish I could talk to him right now.

    Life is good in other ways. I haven't been too sick lately, although this week I did have a cold with a fever. I felt run-down, and then no Valentine from Jessie! I sent him one on the 10th. Work was fun, making Valentines with the children. Seminary was fun, too. I made the first cuts to be hired full time. They only take 8 people out of 40. I feel honored that I made it this far. I am learning a lot. So much in my life is good. My family has been so supportive of me—everyone, especially my mom and my little niece Ella. She is always so sweet to me and tells me I'm pretty. I love her and all of my family. They are great. I just want to settle my feelings about Jessie. I feel so upset right now. Life is difficult, too—especially when you are afraid of having your heartbroken. I just don't know what will happen. It all seemed fine last Saturday. I don't know why it is different. Well, I am thankful for journals so that I can get my feelings out at least.

                  Love,

                  Nancy

That night, after I wrote in my journal, as I was saying my prayers, I prayed from my heart to my Heavenly Father to help me. Then I read my scriptures. As I was falling asleep, a question I had asked Him was answered. I had asked Him, "Heavenly Father, What am I to learn from this?"

The thought came into my mind and heart, "I want you to first trust in me, and other supports will be there. I want you to know that you can go through this without Jessie because you can lean on me." I felt comforted by this knowledge that the Lord expected me to lean on Him. Even though Jessie had been someone I had felt comfortable leaning on, I would still be fine, even if his support was not there anymore. I needed that knowledge more than anything. I fell asleep, thankful for a kind and loving Heavenly Father who is always there for me. I knew it was time to let go of my attachment to Jessie and to see what would happen. I felt sad and confused because just last week it had all seemed so good with him. But I just had to wait and see how things would work out.

Chapter 21

Relationships

I had planned to ski the next day at Deer Valley. I went skiing with my friend Leslie. Skiing really helps me to appreciate and love life. We had a great time. Although I did okay for a cancer patient, I was pretty tired at the end of the day. Time continued to fly by with my busy schedule. On February 28, I wrote in my journal:

Dear Journal,   February 28, 1990

Well, I am finally starting my new journal now that I have filled up my mission journal three and a half years past my mission in Hong Kong. Life is good right now. I am still receiving chemotherapy, and the radiation is done. I am not teaching seminary anymore because I got cut from the last eight. I guess I should feel honored that I made it as far as I did. It was a good experience, but because of my perfectionist ways, I somehow feel that I failed. Yet I know that rejection is not failure. Maybe I did succeed in some small way. I hope I did. My work is going well. I'm totally caught up with my paperwork. I feel successful with my relationships with my coworkers and the patients. Life is really good.

As far as Jessie goes, I haven't really heard from him lately. I guess I have to accept it. I want him to be there, but it is more important for him to go on a mission than it is for him to love me. I really believe that. I know how important missions are, and I just want him to be happy first. I really do love him; I think I've bonded with him because of this experience so much more than if I had not had cancer. He has given me some good memories of playfulness in the midst of a crisis, so I only have good feelings for him.

As for my cancer treatments, my right breast is really tan from the radiation, and I have sharp, short-lived pains and some nausea, but not much. I've lost about twelve pounds since the surgery, but it is great because I can now fit in my skinniest jeans, so I feel OK. I'm not really scared of any reoccurrences of the cancer. I feel pretty confident about it; I hope rightfully so.

Matt called me the other night from California. He was made a priest in the Aaronic Priesthood. He sounded very happy, and he said he sometimes takes his five-year-old brother to church with him. He also said his parents cannot believe he has changed so much, and they now feel that they can trust him. He said he is doing well in school, and he wants to get good grades so he can go to college. He also has a job. He wants me to come and visit as soon as I can. I will. His mother said she would pick me up at the airport. Sometimes it is amazing to me that I can have a close relationship with a 16-year-old boy. I do love Matt like a son or little brother. Either way, he feels like family. He is great. I also feel close to Monica, Meri, Amy, and others who are only 17 years old. Then, of course, Jessie is also only 19 (although he does seem older to me). He has a lot of good qualities that I admire like his compassion for others and his ability to communicate. I will close for now. Life is good. I wish I could talk to Jessie right now.

That's all for now

Love, Nancy

Chapter 22

Path to recovery

I was concerned about my health, and I had tried to eat healthy, but it was difficult when only certain foods sound good. I did force myself to eat my fruits and vegetables when I could tolerate them. Yet, strangely, I sometimes felt very energetic.

Lately, it seemed that I wanted to try everything I had always wanted to do but for some reason had never done. For example, I used to enjoy being in theater in high school and in college. Although, I had never had a major role—just smaller parts; I'd always wished I could get a bigger part. I usually danced and sang in the chorus. While I was looking into a special theatre program for a boy patient at my work, I learned that they also had adult classes. I decided to take the class. It was only one night a week. We did monologues and sang. I particularly enjoyed the singing. I had always been in choir, and I had sung in church choirs. This was more like group voice lessons with some acting.

I also took a tap class at the Park City Racquet Club, and I was doing aerobics every morning at my friend Jeannie's house before work at about 7:15 a.m. She lived three minutes from my house. We knew each other from Long Beach. Actually, she was from Seal Beach next to Long Beach, and she had come to Park city to ski and married a pro golfer; they made their home in Park city. Jeanine and I had met at a church girl's camp many years ago as teens. She was so happy and upbeat; I loved starting my day with her doing aerobics.

After our work outs, I'd then go home, shower, and be to work between nine or ten. It took me about thirty minutes to get to work. I was just doing everything that I had always wanted to do, but for some reason, had not yet done in my life. Time seemed to be much more valuable to me now, I filled it with things I always wanted to do, and it was fun!

On March 23rd I wrote the following entry in my journal.

Dear Journal,   March 23, 1990

It's been too long since I wrote again. My life is still going strong. I'm still on chemotherapy, and I am involved in a performing arts school on Wednesday nights for four hours of vocal and acting coaching. It's great. I also take a jazz tap class on Thursday nights. It's really fun—I even bought tap shoes! I work out to Jane Fonda at my friend Jeanine's house before work for an hour every morning. I am working full time and am going out on the weekends with friends. It doesn't sound like I have cancer, does it? It is just what I like. The energy is there for some reason, so, I keep busy. But, now, I think I have a cold, so I have to slow down. Because I felt dizzy and weak yesterday, I didn't go to my jazz tap class or aerobics this morning. I was told not to go by the doctor. Life is good though. Jessie is coming to visit me April 11-15, around Easter. I am really excited to see him again.

Also, my childhood friend Robin was here to visit me last week. We went cross-country skiing two times, went to church and Temple square, and I gave her another Book of Mormon since she lost the last one I gave her. She is a very dear friend, more like a sister. We had fun sightseeing, and we took lots of pictures.

I have also talked to Matt; he is now in the presidency of the Aaronic Priesthood and is very active in the Church. He is such a sweetheart and someday will be a great missionary. I hope Jessie will also go on a mission. It will be in his time, though. It can't be forced. I think about marrying him. I hope I get to someday, but I don't know for sure if it will happen. All I know is that I love him. He's the best guy I know. He's supposed to call me today at 10:30 a.m., my time. I'm excited. That is all for now. I am thankful for my family, friends, Christ, and the gospel. Bye,

Love Nancy

Going to church has always been a part of my life. During my treatments it seemed that I received much emotional and spiritual support while going through this trial. Two days later, on March 25, 1990, I wrote the following.

Dear Journal,

Well, hi. Life is still good. I'm thankful for my health so much. Today in sacrament meeting a man bore his testimony. He only had one arm due to an accident. His testimony was very inspiring. He has had a lot of trials in his life. He was divorced 12 years ago and has a 14-year-old son. I was impressed with his courage in life. I also listened to the testimony of a young girl who had been in a serious car accident. The doctors had only given her a 6-percent chance of living. She didn't even have a scar that could be seen, and she bore a beautiful testimony of her appreciation for life. I felt close to these testimonies because I, too, felt thankful for life after surgery. It has changed me to try new things and think of others more. In fact, in many ways I feel like I haven't suffered much at all. I loved being at church today and felt proud that I was able to serve a mission and represent Christ's church. I am so proud of the gospel of Jesus Christ and its good people who strive to live by His teachings. I am thankful for my family, friends, and especially Jessie. I hope he goes on a mission soon. He really is a gifted person, and I hope he can learn to use his gifts in building the kingdom of God. That is what we are here for— the very purpose of life. I hope he learns this. I do love him. I'm excited that he is coming to visit in 17 days. It will be so fun having him here.

Today was a good Sabbath Day. My friend Karen and I got together for dinner and to watch a movie on TV. We watched Hemingway's The Old Man and the Sea. I also took a nap today because I haven't had that much energy lately. Karen is a good friend. I like her quirky sense of humor. Tomorrow I want to ski again.

I try not to feel sorry for myself, but lately sometimes it is hard. My hair is falling out, and often I find myself looking at other girls' full beautiful hair. That is when Jessie gives me strength. He doesn't even seem to care that my hair is falling out at all. It feels great to think that someone loves you regardless of the outside appearance. He seems to love me because I'm me. It feels so good. I know my Heavenly Father loves me that way, as well as my Earthly parents. Life really is good. I love it. I love Park City, though I do miss the beach in California. I can't wait to go again.

Love, Nancy

Chapter 22

Drug-induced euphoria and trying to enjoy life

Some days life was good, and I'm sure that it was because of how I chose to spend my day. Working hard and playing hard. I think sometimes my life was one big surge of adrenaline during treatment. It almost seemed unnatural, like I was on a stage performing for everyone and everyone was clapping and cheering me on in my performance. During the show, they watched me cry real tears, and laugh on cue. They saw my life unfolding before them and there was no intermission or exits off the stage. I was forever performing to avoid a bad review and to avoid hearing my critics who ever that might be, maybe myself. There was dancing, singing and being a friend to all the supportive loved ones in my life.

It wasn't until later that I found out that the steroid, Dexamethasone, that they were giving me to avoid the nausea had a side effect of euphoria and it was giving me an unnatural energy and enthusiasm for life. I unknowingly, had yet to truly deal with effects of having cancer. I thought to myself when I learned this... "Hmm so when will I feel the effects?"

One weekend, after my treatment, my family had a family reunion with the Smith family (Monica's family and Carla my oldest sister's husband's family). Carla's father-in-law (Monica's grandpa) had a big home on several acres with horses. There was a stream stocked with trout to fish in off his dock by the stream and a swimming pool. In the house, he had a pool table and a refrigerator stocked full of candy bars and ice cream for all.

There were a lot of adults and children between the two families. There was an indoor racquet ball court and indoor Jacuzzi too. We enjoyed all the fun; it lasted two days with entertainment by all—singing and dancing too. I sang a duet with my niece and played the guitar; a group of us also sang another song. Ella and I sang a church contemporary song called *In Quiet Grove,* about Joseph Smith's First vision.

I also enjoyed giving swimming lessons to many of the children there. Monica and I had come to visit her grandfather on occasion and had enjoyed swimming there on Friday nights when he would open up his home to all and let us bring any friends we wanted too. A couple of times, I brought a friend, and once I even brought "Little Sean" whom I was assigned to work with. I had also brought little Sarah there before, and she loved swimming there too.

Our families also took a trip to Lake Powell. We all rented a house boat together. It was also fun, although by then my hair had become almost non-existent the only thing that kept me from looking bald was the two weeks between chemo when my hair grew back a little. So I had some wisps of hairs about one inch or so that were new growing in where the old had fallen out. It looked strange. I still had not cut my remaining long hair that was now still pulled back in a pony tail, and the pony tail was only about one sixteenth of an inch in diameter. To me, it was enough hair because I wasn't bald. Even with all the fun, including family reunions, trips to Lake Powell, and skiing, I still wanted to go to California.

My mom was taking a short trip on the weekend to see my great grandpa who was sick, so I decided to go with her. I went along, and it was quick. When I went, I saw Jessie. I sensed problems, and so we talked about it.

"It has to do with the age." he said. I feel like I am not good enough for you because I am younger, and it feels like I don't have that much to offer you." After talking a while he finally said he wished he was older.

    I could understand what he was saying. I think he wants to feel more in control or something. I have always been so independent and have so much pride that I just accept things ending as if they were going to. Why would I want to try to hang on to someone that does not want to have a relationship with me? That just comes from being a single entity for so long. One does not think about more than one person in their plans of their life unless it has been ingrained into them to do so. I had been single, for all of my adult life. That is how I thought; in singularities. I told myself I can help him feel older. I will try. He said that the relationship was very stressful for him. I told myself I would make it better somehow. I still could not completely let go. I thought I needed him too much. The trip was good though. It was good to see my friends in California.

    Jessie and I spent time together at his family's house. We went to the park and played softball together with his brothers and sisters.

    My friend Jennifer and I went to watch Jessie's city league baseball game. He hit a home run at the bottom of the ninth with a runner on base; his team down by one run to win the game. He didn't seem to even look the least bit worried when he was up to bat. He was also the pitcher and struck a few people out. I was impressed, and so was Jennifer. I went home feeling like this could work out, but it probably wouldn't until he was older and had been on a mission. I really thought I loved him.

The next week, I picked him up at the airport. He seemed a little distant, but I wasn't worried because he had already told me what he was feeling. We had an Easter dinner at my parent's house, and we both stayed there at night. Then the week did not go well, but we did communicate about what happened to make our relationship so stressed. It did not seem to be a big problem to me because I knew if this relationship was right it would not really work out to be a serious relationship until later in our lives. He was a great supportive friend to me as I dealt with my cancer, but he was in California. This long distance relationship was far away in more than one aspect for me. Far away in age, distance, and in the fact that nothing would really happen until after his mission. Whatever would happen with us seemed as far away to me as a child's mind perceives their next birthday to be. For me, if you can't see the future and where it is taking you, it is hard to have a plan. My dream of being with him was only a dream and not based on reality for me or him. I guess he was an escape or fantasy during a stressful time for me and definitely not reality.

He left with nothing being certain between us except that we shared a bond of friendship and frustration with life.

Chapter 23

Love of children

The snow had melted in the valley and was beginning to melt in the foothills on the Wasatch front. The noonday sun warmed the brown wet mud by the pond in front of the residential treatment center where I worked. I curled my toes into the mud, and I felt the coolness of the tiny pebbles between my toes.

My residential care center children were playing out by the pond with their homemade paper boats. I sat watching their feet sink into the warm mud as they retrieved their capsized boats from the water. A little boy, who did not like the mud, asked me to help him get his boat from the water. I took one step in the mud and sank down into it. My feet and ankles were covered with mud, and I walked into the water to rescue his now nearly sunken boat. I gave it back to him to dry out in the sun and then went over to the hose and began washing my feet off. Quickly several little muddy feet ran toward me wanting me to squirt their feet clean. I began squirting them off one by one. They squirmed as the water splashed off their boney feet on to their clothes. I felt like starting a water fight, and I teased them that I would spray them even more, but I didn't. Instead I turned off the hose and told them, "Time for lunch. Line up!"

Still receiving my chemo treatments, the smell of the food from the cottage made me nauseated. I could not stand the smell of cooked canned corn. I tried not to show how sick I was feeling from the smell as we had the children sit down for their lunch. The menu was mini frozen pizzas, canned corn, and canned fruit. The dessert was a big chocolate chip cookie that had been bought in bulk. I slid my chair back a little from the table to avoid getting an unwanted whiff of the corn smell as I sat watching the children eat.

My job was perfect for me and very fun because I loved being with the kids and trying to help them progress in their treatment. Each one of them did have a special place in my heart, and I sometimes felt too close to them. So close, I would become too involved.

It was confusing to me because the children needed to learn to bond, but my job relationship should also be a professional relationship. It confused me, because, how does one have a professional relationship with a child and still teach them how to bond like families?

Sometimes I had a hard time working with children because of their vulnerability. I preferred working with teenagers because I felt like they could be held more accountable for their actions. I believed that children could also be accountable, but I felt so much more sorrow for them. It was such a terrible thought to think of all the abuse that some of these children had been through. I struggled emotionally as I frequently heard their cries from the time-out room when the pains of their pasts escaped from within their broken hearts. The cries or wails of the children broke into the inner most rooms of my heart like an international thief breaking into the center of the Louvre, waltzing past the security with ease.

I would reason with my feelings and say that it was not that bad by thinking, I know that these bad things happen in the world whether I work here or not, and they will continue to happen in this world, so even though I cannot stop these things from happening, at least I can possibly help in a small way to make a difference in a child's life somewhere along the way. These were words that comforted me for the moment and gave me the strength to continue working there.

I really did prefer working with adolescents. We did have some children as old as 14 years old, and it was easier for me to work with them because I could teach them to learn from their past mistakes and to learn to be accountable for their own mistakes and not for their parent's mistakes. It wasn't that I couldn't teach the younger ones, but it was that it took so much more out of me emotionally to teach them as opposed to the teenagers.

The children I worked with knew I had cancer. Some of them had lost relatives to cancer and frequently wanted to talk to me about my cancer. They would ask me if I was going to die because their aunt had died from cancer, and they thought I was going to die too.

The children were also concerned about my hair loss. They were afraid that they could get cancer from me and their hair might also fall out. This, at times, was a good thing because they were learning that not everyone dies from cancer. It was not long ago when most people believed that if someone had cancer that it was only a matter of time before they would die. Unfortunately, that is still the case when cancer is caught too late but not if it is caught at the most early stages. I tried to let them know in the simplest way I could that cancer is a part of life and there is a treatment that you take to get rid of the cancer, but even though it can make your hair fall out, that was okay because your hair would grow back.

I have always loved children because I think they have a way of teaching me to look at life with a simplicity that heals me from the complicated, cynical, and caustic ways of some people in the world. I was grateful for the opportunity to be taught by children and for me to try to teach and help them. In all their innocence, sometimes they really can be wise beyond their years. In the Bible it states in the book of Daniel 12:3 "They that be wise shall shine as the brightness of the firmament." I think that children shine. It is the purity in them that makes them shine.

Most of the children that I worked with were alone in the world and were having difficulty learning how to bond or lean on others. Loving comes naturally for children until it is upset by abuse which leads to failed bonding. Bonding is not a skill that comes naturally, but it is a skill that is taught and learned much like learning to ride a bike, and once you learn you never forget. Many of my children at the RTC had not learned how to fully bond with another. They did not have the opportunity to learn it because their mistrust of adults took away their ability to bond. Instead, they developed an attachment disorder.

   At my job, I could lose myself in my work. I loved to read bedtime stories to them and to teach them poetry. It was an art form that allowed them to speak to others and share their perceptions of this fearful unknown world. In writing poetry, they could speak through their own voices, and others could hear them.

   As the snow continued to melt so did my heart as children moved on to a hopefully better life. Little Sean, my assigned child, was adopted into a new family. He was missed by all. I missed the hugging time.

Chapter 24

"DES"

Spring freed my hibernating soul from winter and teased me with sunshine, but winter briskness still loitered in the streets. My treatments were almost over. Each day brought new things to do, and I was trying to make all my moments have meaning. There were always unexpected events that made the road bumpy along the way.

On April 24th 1990 I wrote the following in my journal.

Dear Journal,   April 24th 1990

Today was a scary day. My sister Carol's pap smear came back with signs of pre-cancerous cells, and she will need to get a biopsy done at outpatient surgery. I felt really upset that she has this problem. When I heard the news, I was afraid she might die. She has three children, Dave, age 8, Ella age 7, and Rachel about 4 months. I hope it is nothing. I'm still very scared. I will go to the temple and pray for her in two days. Hopefully it will work out, and she'll be fine.

I haven't heard from Jessie for a long time, and this is strange because I think of him as such a good friend. I really miss him. He needs to focus on his mission anyway. He has plans to go now, but I don't know when. I will be excited to write him when he does. I really love everything about him. I don't know what will happen. Sometimes, I think he is going to hurt me someday, or maybe I will hurt him. I just hope we can be together again someday.

That is all for now. Life is good.

Love, Nancy

One day, I left work on a Friday for chemotherapy treatments, and the doctor always tested my white blood count before they would give me my treatments. I was sitting in the doctor's room waiting to hear the results wondering why it was taking so long. He then came in and told me that my white blood count was too low. "You will not be able to get your treatment today" he said, in a concerned and matter of fact tone. My initial reaction was to worry, but when I noticed he didn't seem too concerned, I quickly calmed down. He said that my body just needed a rest, and we would try again next week. He talked to me and let me know that he thought my prognosis was good. He also told me that in 1989 breast cancer had gone up 29% in women in my age bracket, and no one knows why. I asked him if it could be because of the number of woman who took DES in the 1950's and 1960's during their pregnancy. He said there had been no studies to his knowledge that link DES to breast cancer, only to cervical cancer. I told him that I had taken a test in a women's magazine that was supposed to tell you how high risk you are for breast cancer. I told him that I was in the 80% according to this test all because I answered yes to the question, "Did your mother take DES when she was pregnant with you?" I told him I had also heard there was a group of women in Los Angeles that ran a support group for women who were DES babies, and I asked him if he had heard of them.

He said, he had not heard of this group, but he supposed it was possible that it could be linked to DES; however, the research had not been done to prove this. (Now the research is currently being done, and it will be interesting to find the results.)

I enjoyed my oncologist's down-to-earth quality and his willingness to talk with me when he had a whole waiting room full of patients. I appreciated good doctors, and I felt like I had some of the best.

As I left the office, I felt a wave of nausea come over me, and I thought to myself, "This is weird, I didn't even get my treatment, and yet I still feel nauseated." The mind is so powerful. It must be my mind playing tricks on me, and I tried to make it go away so I could go back to work.

Chapter 25

Letting go of the hair loss

Time flew by and on June 13th I wrote in my journal the following entry:

Dear Journal,

It's been way too long as usual. It's June 13, 1990 today. Life is still going strong. My sister Carol had minor surgery. They took out part of her cervix that had pre cancerous cells. She's fine. She was at her son's baseball game the next day. Missy, my other younger sister had to have exploratory surgery because she might have a cyst on her ovaries, so never a dull moment. Oh yes, and my parents were in a bad car accident too. Their car flipped completely over, and they were found by a highway patrol car upside down sitting in their seatbelts waiting for someone to come along and find them. They didn't have a scratch on them because they were wearing their seat belts. Seat belts saved their lives, or it just wasn't yet their time to go. I can't even imagine what it would have been like if they had not survived.

I still think about Jessie; although he never really calls, at least I have the fun memories that we had together to remember. He still doesn't have his mission call, and he has lots of reasons why that seem valid so he may not go right away. That will be hard because if we ever were to get together then it will be that much longer we will have to wait. I miss him, and sometimes I am lonely, but I also know he is not the right person for me, I think. I am going to California this month, June 23rd- 26th. I hope we can have some time together and spend some time with his family. I enjoyed spending time with them last time. Well life goes on and the future can be prosperous, I know it! Whatever happens!

Thanks for journals!

Love, Nancy

The chemotherapy is finally done. It feels a little insecure because I won't be going to the doctor much, only for a few checkups this year. I am happy, but I will also have to adjust my life to life after the adrenaline rush of having cancer. It is like your goal of fighting cancer for the last few months has just dissipated. It is like you want to put closure on this, but how does one put closure on cancer so you don't? At least you don't, not yet, and not easily.

Even if you are cured, and I think I am, this experience will always be part of me, and I am not sure I want to put closure on it. If I do, does that mean I am not acting responsible, if I forget I ever had cancer? No, I cannot do that. Do I run away from all that reminds me of this experience? No, because if I did I would be denying who I am. I am now a cancer survivor. This does not mean that I do not worry that it will come back again, because I do. It was not a welcomed guest before, and I do not plan to welcome it back. But if it does come back, I do hope that I will be better at dealing with it so that I will shine on that stage next time—if there has to be another time. I hope next time I can step off the stage into more reality and really use this experience for all that it is worth. Of course, there are other ways to learn besides having cancer I will be perfectly willing to utilize those experiences. I am a cancer survivor, and somehow I must overcome; now I am tired of running the race, and I need to rest.

In the beginning of summer, right after I was done with treatments, I went with Amy and friends camping in Moab. I invited Jeannie, and she brought her pop-up trailer which was good because we had a few rain storms while we camped; we all stayed inside when it rained and talked. There were about eight of us women camping together. It was so fun talking with such a great bunch of women. We stayed up talking until late every night and then floated down the river all day, and I was so relaxed. I had such a good time.

My hair when it was growing in new hair and still had some of the old hair.

In my journal, I finally was done resting and wrote on August 26th 1990 the following.

Dear Journal,   August 26th 1990

Well the rest of the whole summer has come and gone. It has really been a rough summer for me. Lots of trials, and I just didn't feel like writing. I have been sick a lot this summer with colds and flu. I had 8 cavities too, and I never have cavities. I guess it is common after chemo. I still have hair on my head, but it has been radically changed, and I feel the loss every day. I have always loved my long hair, and I think a lot of myself esteem has been based on my appearance. I had to cut my hair short since it started growing back in. It's real short. I feel like I look like a boy, but I got some styling gel and a perm—it doesn't look too bad, I guess. A lot of people say they like it. Unfortunately I haven't liked it much. In fact, I doubt the truthfulness of their statements saying it looks good, and instead, it is just their kindness saying it looks good, but maybe it is just me being insecure.

I have also had a lot of problems with this girl at work—constant conflict with responsibilities and work habits. It has been almost a nightmare for me, but I am learning to handle situations of conflict with others. It seems I handle conflicts with things like cancer better than I do with difficult people. Life is hard sometimes, and I am having a hard time.

My social life is null, but part of that is my own fault because I am not going out with my friends; I am always too tired or sick plus my hair insecurities. I've gained some weight, and I feel fat too. I need to start exercising again. I did so well when I was on my chemo, now I feel like my life is falling apart.

Actually, I'm still fighting to works things out. I am fighting with work problems, exercise, social life and everything. I've been to California a few times this summer.

When I went the first time, I met Jessie at his baseball game, and I got my heart broken because he had another girl there with him. He tried to hide it from me because I was sitting in the stands with two of my friends, and we were leaving early to go to my sister Carla's house. I guess he thought he could pull it off because his girlfriend would just blend in with the rest of the coed team. I could feel something was wrong, and I felt very hurt by the way he was acting. The next day he called me, and I told him I didn't want to see him the rest of my trip. I was very hurt, and I am still hurt. We've talked a few times since then, yet it will never be the same between us. He still hasn't left on his mission, but he is sending in his papers. I am glad that he wants to go. He will be a good missionary. He never calls me anymore. Yet when we have run into each other in California, he always acts like he is planning on calling me, but I don't believe him anymore. It is over, and it has taken sometime to feel better about this. Lesson learned hopefully—maybe my heart was not broken as much as my ego badly bruised. I think I sometimes set up my relationship attachments as my fuel for my superficial focus on my looks—feeding my ego. Not good!

Some things in my life are happy; like my nieces and nephews are fun, and Matt is doing great. I went to church with Matt while I was in California, and he was participating in the sacrament ceremony. He has grown so much, I really love him. He is such a good friend. I do have lots of good friends. I have got to go now, I am going to hear Jon, one of my Sunday school students, give his farewell address before he goes to Switzerland on his mission. I am not teaching the Primary boys anymore, but instead, I am team teaching the high school Sunday school class with my good friend, Marian. It will be great to hear Jon speak. He is a great guy. Bye for now,

Love, Nancy

Chapter 26

New California job

I had been thinking about moving back to California, My mom said that she thinks I would not be able to do this because of my insurance. She said that if I change insurance, my cancer check-ups won't be covered, and if I were to have a reoccurrence that it would be considered pre-existing. This made me feel like my cancer was going to force me to live only in Utah and force me to only work at the same job. I felt like this must be wrong, so I started to look into insurance policies and found that most of them in their preexisting clause stated that in order for it to be covered you would have to not be seen by a doctor for this problem for at least six months. I was only seeing my doctors every six months now so this would not be a problem for me if I decided to move.

After we talked through the problems, things got better at work. I was enjoying my job now. However, I was still searching for closure to this whole experience called cancer.

Whenever I needed peace in my life as a younger person, I would go to the beach, and I missed living close to the ocean. As an older person, I would go to the temple to find peace and strength to deal with my problems, and I was going to the temple now but still felt like I needed to move. I did want to get away from it all, and the beach was my place of choice to escape.

I was asking myself, as I would buy an LA Times in the Park City grocery store each week and search the classified ads for Recreational Therapy jobs, "Am I running away from my cancer memories, or am I making a sound decision to move?"

There were so many constant reminders of the cancer. For example, sometimes when I went downtown to run an errand for work and my destination took me past the Salt Lake clinic, I would feel nausea come on again. It did not take long for it to subside, but just the same, it amazed me that the mind was so powerful that just looking at the building where I received all that chemotherapy could make me feel the same exact type of nausea and smell the familiar smells of the inside of the building.

After searching for a California job for a couple months, I found a few job possibilities, but nothing that worked from all angles. There was one job located further down south in

Southern Orange County closer to my sister, Carla, my great grandfather, and my great aunt. The private psychiatric hospital was right on a cliff overlooking the ocean. I would be working mostly with adolescents and some adults. I was really excited when they called me back, but when we finally talked, I found out that they could only offer me a part-time job right now. They hoped it would turn into a full-time with benefits soon. I just didn't feel that I could take something without benefits because I would have to go on the cobra plan of my current insurance and the premiums would take a huge chunk of my part-time pay check. Reluctantly, I did not take the job. I did tell them that if they ever had a full-time job, I would love to be considered for the position.

    I finally found a job working as a Recreational Therapist with adolescents in Long Beach downtown. Most of the kids I would be working with at the center were mainly inner city LA kids. This company contracted with the state of California to provide psychiatric services for adolescents. The program was the last stop for treatment before the adolescents were considered sick enough for the state hospital. They offered me the job. They had the Kaiser Permanente insurance plan, a very big southern California

HMO. My friend's mother had cancer a few years ago, and she had Kaiser Insurance. She was still living, so I thought this might not be so bad. I knew I had some great doctors caring for me here, but I also did not want to base all my decisions on which doctor would care for me if I were to ever get cancer again, which I hoped would never happen anyway.

I called my friend, Michelle's mother, and found out about the doctors at Kaiser. Her mother said she really liked her doctor and recommended him to me. I called the office, and he would be able to see me near the first of the year, a little after six months since the last time I saw my doctors in Utah elapsed.

It all fell into place. I shared a room in an apartment with Michelle and April. Our rent was cheap. They were happy to have me. Michelle, who I would be sharing a room with, was having financial problems and would have to move home. Now with my help in the rent, she did not have to move home. They were fun roommates. I had met them at church about three years ago before I moved to Utah.

My mom told me that Michelle's mother used to babysit me when I was about 3 years old. I thought this is a small world. I was excited about my new job and was ready for the move. The money was only about the same I was making in Utah—even though the California cost of living would be a lot more. It was okay because I didn't mind having roommates; I enjoyed them.

The Christmas holidays were pleasant, and another Christmas party at the residential treatment center came and went. I loved Christmas a lot, but I was thinking a lot about moving. I gave my notice at work, and I think they expected it with all my frequent trips to California. It would be hard to move on; but it felt right, and I would miss the good people at the RTC.

More than a year had passed since I was officially diagnosed with cancer. After Christmas, I moved back to my hometown and began to settle into my old and new life. I was excited to spend time with all my old friends in California, but I would miss my new friends in Utah.

Chapter 27

Struggling with weight gain & low self-esteem

On January 6th 1991, I wrote the following in my journal.

Dear Journal,

Guess what! I've moved to California. It's been a long time since I've written in you. A lot has happened. Some great things have happened! I'll write a little each day, try to fill you in, and try to catch you up.

First, I took a job at an adolescent treatment center, 50-bed-hospital in Long Beach. I love the job. I love the kids. I live with April and Michelle. I love my roommates. Life is good. I have only seen Jessie once, and it was by accident. I guess I've been avoiding him because I still don't look my best with my short hair and my weight gain. Plus, he never calls. We have accidently talked on the phone a few times when I called his grandmother. He answered the phone, so I took the opportunity to encourage him to go on a mission.

He was excited to tell me that he got his mission call to Brazil. I have a friend who is in Brazil on a mission now, and

I told him I would give him my friend's address so that he could learn more about the Brazilian way of life.

He seemed excited to go on his mission. I am also excited for him. I was feeling kind of bad because he never even called me, especially about his mission. I only found out when I called his grandparents.

I guess he is too young for me; I should basically stay away from him. Besides, he has a girlfriend now, and last Sunday, he baptized her into the church. His grandparents invited me to go, but I had a good excuse. I had to work. Besides, up until that time, I had not even seen him since last spring when he brought the girlfriend to the baseball game. I was scared to see him because of how I would feel. I looked fat. For some reason, I have been real self conscious of how I look. At least I have still been having fun with my friends since I moved here.

Anyway, this week, I accidently saw him at a church activity. He came to the same activity with a friend. When he saw me he said, "Hi" and gave me a hug. He then introduced me to his friend Jon as Mary Gibson. He called me my mother's name! I was angry. I don't know, maybe he was nervous, he acted real strange, but it did hurt me. I told him that I was happy to hear that he was able to baptize his girlfriend. He said, "Thanks." It felt very awkward to be talking to him. I told him I was planning to come to his mission farewell. He had told me another day on the phone when his mission farewell was. That day he had said, "Mark that day on your calendar hint, hint." I assumed that meant he wanted me to go to his farewell. I guess I wasn't sure what he meant. For awhile I wasn't sure if I would go to his farewell, but I then realized that I needed to forgive him, show some support, and just let go of my hurt and anger. Maybe he does care if I go or not. It just doesn't seem like he cares. Oh yes, I forgot to mention that here I was worried about how I looked with my very short hair and my weight gain, and when I saw him he had gained weight too. Quite a bit, so, I shouldn't have worried because if he really loved me, he wouldn't care as long as I was still healthy. I still loved him when I saw him even though he had gained weight. There were just too many strong memories for me to have only a superficial attachment to him. I was glad to see that I did love him not just for his physical attributes. I was glad to see I loved him for the right reasons, not just for his looks.

I wanted to tell you that before I moved I went to visit little Sarah and her new family. They wanted to thank me for all that I had done for her in the past while she was at Primary Children's hospital. They invited me to their home any time, and I invited them to visit me in California. They said they might take me up on that. It looks like little Sarah might get another one of her wishes come true. I might get to take her to the beach after all. I haven't any children of my own, but I have all my nieces, nephews, Sarah, Sean and Matt. I feel like I am a mother. I love my job, my life, and all of my many blessings. I love missionary work too.

Love, Nancy

Over all, my life was not that bad. Nevertheless, I was still very focused on my weight gain. I had been trying to take this weight off, but my metabolism is all messed up because of my treatments. I realized that because I wasn't eating that much during my treatment, I had lost my appetite, and my metabolism had slowed way down to survive. The steroids they had me on to keep me from getting too sick also caused weight gain, so I really had the cards stacked against me.

When the side effects of euphoria from the drugs had worn off, I felt tired and depressed from everything, and I wasn't exercising. I was tired from all I had just gone through, and my metabolism was crawling at the pace of a snail from not eating. About the time I got my appetite back and food suddenly sounded good to me again, it seemed that all I had to do is be in the same room with a piece of chocolate cake and I'd gain 10 pounds. This was not fair. I had worked so hard to fight this like a trooper, and now I have to end this battle being bald and fat yet alive. This was so hard to fight another battle with my body because I had just finished fighting one. I did not want to feel ungrateful, but I did not like this at all. Being single and being in the world of trying to get dates while I was having permanent bad hair and now being over-weight on top of it did not seem fun to me. I started to believe that not only was life unfair, but it certainly was not fun. I guess I had to take on this challenge and try to find a way back to a healthier me.

Now I had to find a way to take off the pounds to get back my old body. I didn't mind the scars from the surgery, and my scars were not visible except for when I wore a bathing suit. They were located under my arm (where they took out the lymph nodes). My scars didn't bother me at all. As a matter of fact, I was kind of proud of my scars because I felt that having cancer was not easy, and I had done something good to learn how to overcome the hardship of cancer. Because I was proud of myself and also wanted to be proud of my body, I decided to start running again. It was discouraging at first because the weight did not come off fast enough for me. I still had about twenty-five to thirty pounds to lose. Sometimes it seemed like an impossible task and was very discouraging. Yet I tried not to let it get me down and was still able to have fun with my friends.

Chapter 28

Valuing life—The Iraq War

It was easy in my new job. I was staying up late, and I did not have to be at work until 1:00 pm. I was sleeping in and trying to exercise—but did not always do it when I knew I should. There seemed to be some sort of dark cloud over my head, and at times, I felt kind of lethargic. I began to wonder if I made the right decision coming to California. This whole cancer experience was supposed to teach me something. I was supposed to be learning to value life, and although I clung to the thought that I was winning the battle, yet the victory did not seem happy nor did I feel victorious. During this battle, I was always saying I will not let my cancer fight make me bitter, only better. And sometimes it felt like 'bitter' was winning.

One morning, I woke up, turned on the TV, and watched the news. The deadline for the Iraq and Kuwait war was counting down. I began to cry, and it was a sobbing type of crying. I was alone in my apartment. Michelle and April were at school and work. The newscaster said that if the deadline for Iraq to get their troops out of Kuwait passes we will go to war. CNN had 24-hour coverage on this and it was the first war coverage I had ever watched. I felt so close to it. I thought to myself, it is very strange and so real. It's not anything like reading about it after the fact. I strongly felt the anticipation and anxiety of the world, particularly that of the servicemen and their families. The newscaster kept talking about the many threats of terrorism that could happen. I thought of the children of the world and how they should not have to be part of a war in any sense, particularly to be living within a war. A very real darkness was settling into me as it seemingly did to the world as well.

I wrote in my journal the next day.

Dear Journal,

I don't believe in war, and I am watching the protesters across the nation demonstrating the UN deadline for Iraq to leave Kuwait. I wish I knew the answer. I feel like it won't hurt to extend the time to avoid war. I also know that leaders such as Saddam Hussein should not be allowed to take over a country no more than cancer should be allowed to take over a body. Then again, perhaps the fight was needed.

I wrote in my journal on January 15, 1991 while I watched the Iraq and Kuwait beginning.

Dear Journal,

Today is a very scary and sad day. It is the deadline President Bush and the Senate, or actually the UN, set for Saddam Hussein to get the Iraqi troops out of Kuwait or else go to war. Everyone is very anxious tonight and very scared. There are many threats of terrorism that might take place. Yes, even here in the "Good Ole" safe USA. I have felt a sense of fear, and now, a new understanding of why we need to have an emergency plan in place. I feel a new sense of urgency. The truth is I am scared. I suddenly feel a real need to be close to my Savior, Jesus Christ and Heavenly Father. I am sad for the children of the world and for the families of those children. I am scared for the soldiers and serviceman all around the world. I am afraid of the effects that war will have on the young people of America. Tonight cities across the nation have Anti-war demonstrations with thousands of demonstrators. I don't believe in war. Although I am anti-war, I believe that we are deeply involved in this problem. I believe that any act of injustice such as a country that tries to overtake another country by force and violence is wrong. It is similar to as if there were a bully in the schoolyard and nobody stood up against the bully; the lack of action could be considered a contribution to bullying by allowing it to happen. If a country bullies, then they need to answer to rest of the world.

I don't think we should go to war because of a deadline though. I believe we should give it more time. Avoid war if at all possible. We, the American people are not really used to war, at least on our own turf, so to speak. If they play by the terrorist rules, it could end up on our turf. What if they act here in L.A.? It could happen. Lives could be lost. I feel like I will be protected for some reason. I am scared. I needed to write in my journal or even talk to someone. Life is so hard, but I will learn from all this. I hope I can be strong and help others along the way.

Well, today is the birthday of Martin Luther King Jr. This is very ironic because of a quote he said years ago. I cried when they read this quote on TV today. "Some men look at the world as it is and ask, why? I dream of the world that isn't and ask why not?" So, it is a sad day. Lives will be lost on the battlefield. When will it ever end?

I took my students to a memorial rally in L.A. yesterday for Martin Luther King Jr., and we listened to his speech "I Have a Dream." There was a whole auditorium of people, and at the end, we all stood and sang "We Shall Overcome." Many people there with us were the people that were with Dr. King at some of the original marches. It was so powerful, and I cried.

My life is just coasting on auto pilot. I feel like I need some goals. I need something more. I might go back to school for a Master's. I need spiritual goals so that I can grow. Well that's all for now. Thanks for listening journal!

Nancy

The next day I wrote the following about the war.

Dear journal,

On the day after the deadline, we bombed Bagdad, Iraq. Then the next day, Iraq bombed Israel, and they tried to bomb Saudi Arabia but didn't because of the US patriot missile intercepting it. The Gulf war has only been in the sky so far, but we are getting closer to calling in the Army. Then it will become a ground war too. Iraq was bombed again, and now Jerusalem and Tel Avi are all in shelters with gas masks because of the possibility of chemical weapons. So far, we have 7 jet pilots missing in action, one confirmed dead, and he is only 33 years old. I am 33 years old! War is so sad. I guess I have to remember that this world is far from perfect and war is part of this world. I wish so bad it wasn't. I feel so sad. Saddam Hussein has threatened again to use terrorism to fight on the home-front. It is kind of scary, but I don't think he will. Maybe he will. I just don't know. The thought is frightening though. The news is constantly about the war on all the networks. I am going to start praying more. I have not prayed as much as I should lately. Well, I don't have much else to say. I am going to read my scriptures tonight, which is another thing I have not been doing much of lately. I have been trying to help the kids at work to feel calmer and understand all this war stuff. That is all for now. Thanks

    Nancy

Chapter 29

Cherishing friends

On the outside, I was doing okay. On the inside, I was trying to enjoy my new life in California with my new perspective; my post cancer treatment perspective. Everything in my life was really kind of easy. Not much in the way of new challenges, besides my depression (which came sporadically, but frequently). I knew I was just starting to fight my own internal war and make sense of it all.

My moods were so unpredictable. I knew since I had stopped my periods that my hormones were completely out of whack. I was still having some periods, but far from being regular. I told myself, I would learn something from this too.

My paperwork at the new job was so easy compared to my previous positions, so that was not stressful. Going to work was very kick-back to me. The kids were interesting and fun and so were my coworkers. I didn't really like the hours though (Tuesday through Saturday 1:00pm-9:00pm), but because my life was so low stress, it didn't matter that much to me. It seemed that apathy was stepping up to the plate in my life, and I was doing my best to strike him out.

The grey cloud of depression after experiencing cancer seemed to slow my progress of learning to be happy again.

On the plus side, my good friend Jennifer returned home from her mission, for about 6 months now, and it was fun to get all of us together. We had a party for her and me at her house. There were lots of good memories at that house where we had both lived together before my mission (seven years before). Jennifer and I had also lived together after my mission in another house she had bought for a rental before she decided to go on her mission. Jennifer worked as a Mechanical Engineer for Boeing, and they gave her a sabbatical to be able to go on a mission. She was called to Salt Lake City, and she worked on Temple Square where she met people from all over the world. I took friends to temple square while she was on her mission. I even took Matt there, and she bore her testimony to him. Matt was now a leader in his young men's program in his ward. Now, Jennifer was home! Our birthdays are within a few days of each other, and we are the same age too. We decided to have a party. Many old friends came, and it was great to see them.

I wrote in my journal on March 3rd 1991:

Dear journal,

Well a lot has happened. I had my birthday March 2nd, and Jennifer gave me a birthday party. It was really for Jennifer too, but she planned it for me. I told them, "Hey it's Jennifer's birthday too."

I do have the greatest friends in the world. Carol and Frank (her boyfriend), Jennifer and Dave (her boyfriend), Kathy, Deb, Robin, her boyfriend, Mark, Lynn his wife, Dave and Heidi his wife, Bruce and Darcy, and my other friend, Dave and even more. We had a great time. It really felt like a celebration of life for me. They had cake, cookies, and ice-cream sundaes. I need to send thank-you cards for the gifts. I received jewelry, plants, an herb garden, for my kitchen window sill and flowers too. It was a party for royalty. I was thrilled and honored they would do so much for me.

Well, I am 34 years old now, going on 16. No, I hope I am not that bad. Life is good, no, it is excellent!

The best news of all is one week ago the ground war ended in just 80 hours after it started. The Iraqis fled Kuwait, so Kuwait is free. The Iraqi government accepted the UN peace offer, and there is a cease fire. So we are now trying to get back our POWs and send home the troops. Part of the cease fire and peace treaty is dependent upon Saddam Hussein being tried for war crimes. I am so happy the war is over, and I think our country grew a lot from this. People really prayed a lot and became united by the efforts of the soldiers. They are heroes. They are truly heroes that won't be forgotten by me and most of the US. I believe in prayer, and I have also seen MIRACLES in my lifetime. The efforts of the soldiers did create miracles along with the prayers of those at home.

We also received the rain that Southern California needed so desperately, and it is still coming down too. I hope we continue to pray the way our nation has learned to pray recently and stay united!

Months passed, so many things happened. Jennifer became engaged to her boyfriend, Dave. Carol was getting married to Frank. Jessie left on his mission, but came home after a few weeks and eventually married his girlfriend. By then, I was just happy for him, but I did not go to the wedding because I had to work. I needed to find more single friends if I wanted to have a social life that had a potential for meeting my husband.

Chapter 30

Feeling better

I moved to Mission Viejo because I was offered a job at the Acute Psychiatric hospital "by the Sea" down south, and it was full-time. I lived with my friend and a past mission companion, Linda, and her husband Scott. They had a cute baby, James, and I got to play with him a lot. For my job as a recreational therapist, part of the job included twice a week hanging out on the beach with the teenagers, exploring the coastal caves, body surfing, or just sitting in the sun. Needless to say, I was in heaven. It did not last long because, unfortunately, at the hospital family owned business, there was a law suit amongst family members, and my position was done away with just 3 months after I was hired. Oh well, I enjoyed it while it lasted. After that, I went back to Long Beach to work. I house sat for about one month for a friend in Long Beach, and I went back to work part time at my previous job at Harborview Long Beach P/T. I also picked up some additional hours at another hospital in Long Beach. I had to pay cobra insurance, but it was not as much as I thought it would be, so I could make payments financially and still survive. After the house sitting job was done, my sister Carla let me move in with her and her husband and children. I stayed a couple of months at their house; she was living in Orange County. Later, I was able to find a roommate to move in with, and I was offered more hours at my part-time job.

All this time, my hair was growing more, and I was starting to work out more and feel somewhat better. I had also started seeing a therapist. I wanted to make sure I was not falling into self-defeating behaviors, and I needed the extra help to deal with my depression. I also did see a MD doctor to try to figure out what was happening with my hormones; all they could do was offer an anti-depressant which I took for a very short time—hated it.

After being temporarily laid off again at my Long Beach job, I made ends meet by working at my adolescent treatment center job. While I was there, a friend the Director of Education had breast cancer. She was amazingly brave. It was in 17 of the 24 of her lymph nodes tested. She was so positive yet kept working like I did. She invited me to go out with some ladies she met at a support group. So I had lunch with a group of breast cancer survivors. I mostly listened and learned as they shared their stories.

I also started taking a Marine biology class at Cabrillo Museum. There was a test after the class, and if I passed, I could be a curator on the whale watch boats for school children and tourists. I was so excited to do this. I passed the test and went out with groups and taught them about the California grey whale and other marine life in Southern California. Being out on the ocean gave me so much joy and peace.

While I worked at my Long Beach acute Psychiatric Hospital job and the Adolescent treatment center job in Long Beach, my Great Grandfather, Roy Shields was dying. He was in his 90's. His heart was weak. I had many childhood memories of him when we visited his avocado ranch in Fallbrook near Oceanside. I visited him in the hospital. Because I had written his life history for a class in college, I knew a lot about him. He was a farmer from Arkansas, and he grew big watermelons. He moved to L.A. long ago during the Great Depression to sell shoes because he said, "People needed shoes, even in the Depression." I said my goodbyes to my grandpa while all our family visited in December.

At work, there was a young patient who was a sailor on a ship docked in Long Beach. He was depressed and stayed a long time at the hospital where I worked. I bonded with him and tried to help him. He looked like my grandpa as a young man. The patient was from Wisconsin. One day, I brought watercolors for him to paint, and he started painting beautiful pictures. I asked him to teach me too. I saw that the process of painting was healing him. Using the medium of watercolor to create seemed to have a power that lifted his depressed spirit. As I painted with him, it was doing the same for me. I thought I should take an oil painting class later, and I did. I discovered a hidden talent and my new love of painting.

During this time, I also read a self-help book *Feeling Good* by David Burns that taught me how to look at my self-defeating thinking and behaviors and to re-evaluate my thoughts to be more rational. After exercise, therapy, painting, being out to sea, seeing many whales and working on my weaknesses, my life was changing. I think it took that long for the residual effects of all the chemotherapy I had put in my body to leave it completely. Month by month, I was slowly starting to feel better.

I still remember the exact moment I started to feel better—back when I was walking down the hall at my part time Recreational Therapy job in Long Beach. All of a sudden, I stopped, and it was as if a gray cloud moved from over my head and the sun was shining on me. I felt the best I had felt in a long time. I even got asked out that week by a co-worker much younger than I, of course. I went out with him, but it was not really that enjoyable. He was just not interesting to me.

Chapter 31

Overcoming depression

Soon my old employer at a hospital that I worked for in 1983, before my mission, and again after my mission in 1986, hired me, again, for a third time (1992). I worked with some of my previous coworkers including Deb whom was my new boss. I loved her! The job paid good money and was in a nice location too, near Long Beach.

I became good friends with all my co-workers, and we had so much fun at work. We all became close like a family. I would take trips back to Utah to see my family, Sarah and Sean, as well as to ski, now that I had money again. I even took a trip to Washington DC with one of my co-workers, Carolyn. We went to the Smithsonian and many other sights. We visited and stayed with a friend from my mission and a childhood friend of Carolyn's too.

Life was moving faster after my counseling, going out on the whale watch boats, and now my painting. My art class had only 3 students. The teacher was a local artist, and she taught us in her garage. I remember painting my first oil painting —a seascape. It was very therapeutic to feel the cool cement beneath my bare-feet and to hear the sound of birds chirping with a Southern California soft ocean breeze blowing into the open garage door. I really was feeling better.

I wrote in my journal on December 10, 1991:

Dear Journal,

I don't think I have told you, but I think I should really be proud of myself because recently I have been trying to become a happier person and to be the best I can be. It all started since the cancer, the chemotherapy, and all that stuff, I was really struggling. I had normal ups and downs, but the downs were getting longer and the ups weren't very enjoyable anymore. Life was very difficult. I was depressed. Now that I am out of that phase of my life, I can talk about it more easily. During that time it was difficult and I was embarrassed to admit how I felt. Sometimes I really did not want to live. It is ironic that someone who lived so beautifully while fighting cancer could change so drastically to wish they could just die. A lot has happened to me in this past year and a half. I am grateful I had this experience. I have really learned a lot. For the last 6 months or so, I have been seeing a therapist about 2 times a month. She has been very helpful and a good listener. I really needed help, and even after the depression has gone, I am still learning a lot about myself. I guess the best way I can summarize what I am learning is that I am learning to be the best I can be, to reach for my dreams, and believe in myself more. This week's session, I discovered something about myself. Sometimes when I am starting to feel successful at something, I hold back or put on the brakes because somewhere in my past I have learned that my role is to be more of a caretaker of others—something which I do believe is of ultimate importance—but not in a fantasy sort of caretaker role that I have set up for myself. In my fantasy, I see my own success as the failure of others. I feel guilty for not allowing others to always have the limelight. It has been my role to not be the one to shine in my accomplishments. I somehow felt confining myself to not outshine others was my way of being loveable to others and accepted. It sounds a little confusing, but the feelings were there to back it up while I talked about this with my therapist. So, I believe that I have done this in my life. My feelings at that moment were sadness primarily because I had not yet been able to accomplish my goals of wanting to be a writer and a competent responsible person who has something to offer others. Some wisdom, perhaps, that is unique to me is that I am able to give to others. I want to develop a creativity that I have within myself, and then I can 'create' just for the sole purpose of pleasing myself.

In my fantasy of being the ultimate caregiver, I have never allowed myself to create just for the sole purpose of enjoying my own talent. I'd never allowed myself to feel that I was a talented person who could create. Anyway, I have these feelings of sadness because I am holding back, and I have guilt for wanting more. Somehow I have developed a fear of succeeding because I am afraid I might hurt others in the process. In my fantasy of care-giving, I have deprived myself of using the one resource in life that will help bring me the strength to really give to others as well as to myself at the same time. My TALENTS! This resource that I have not allowed myself to develop is none other than ME. That is still hard for me to say because when I say ME it sounds selfish, but I have got to get past that perspective because the resource ME is the best gift I can give to others. To really be me is to write, paint, play, set goals, care for others, pray, believe in the highest of values that is to love, create and to educate myself and others to live to the fullest. I deserve to be the best 'me', therefore, I should not cheat myself. Actually, when I cheat myself because of my guilt, I cheat others because I don't show the best side of me and who I really am. Even as I write this, I find myself wanting to hold back, or I feel like maybe I don't know what I am talking about. Now I am starting to ignore my inner self doubt and start believing I can do it. This all sounds so cliché, but it really isn't. This is a turning point in my life. At least, I want it to be. I hope I can leave the fantasy behind that I need to be there for others at the expense of my own progression by abandoning my own dreams. I want to write, paint, sing, serve others, with the very best me there is; and I will not hold back anymore. If I believe in God first, and always remember I am a child of God, which means I have inherited Godlike characteristics of creativity, and love, I can more powerfully believe in myself. I am a daughter of both loving Heavenly parents and Earthly parents who want me to succeed and be the best me I can be. This will help me to remember my divine nature as a child of

God. So as you can see, I am learning and growing first from the cancer and then from the depression. It has all helped me.

They say that through our trials, we become stronger. A man at church was bearing his testimony today. His wife is dying of cancer. He said something I will always remember about trials. He said without trials, there would be no learning, no joy, no miracles, no faith, and no freedom to choose. Trials are really what this life is all about. So our job is to learn from everything we can and then share it with others. Well, I think I have written enough for now. I am really going to write in here more often to help get my life in order. That's all for now.

Thank you for journals.

Nancy

Everything in my life was going better now. It was now going on three years since I finished my chemotherapy treatments, and I was enjoying my new job and friends.

Chapter 32

Broken leg

Shortly after I started my new job, a new trial came. I was in Utah skiing and broke my leg severely in two places while going off a jump. It was a double TIB/FIB spiral fracture. My mom drove me home from Utah where I had been skiing after a night's stay in the hospital in Utah, and it was casted when we got to California by my doctors at Kaiser. The Santos's stepped up as always and took care of me for 2 weeks while I could not get out of bed.

I eventually had a bright pink glow-in-the-dark full leg cast. Although I had to go on disability for a while, I was in bed for 3 weeks with my leg elevated, but they held my job. I went back to work as quickly as I could. My friends from my job visited me and told me not to worry about my job.

Matt also came to visit me. He was now in college and trying to decide if he would serve a mission for the church. I remember Matt drove me to the beach one night after I could get up with crutches, and we walked down the pier. It was so nice to be at the beach. I could not drive with my cast. I think the conversation went like this.

Matt said, "I really want to serve a mission, but I don't know surfing makes me so happy. When I am out there, you can't imagine the high I get from just being out there and then when you catch a wave it is such pure happiness."

I replied, "Matt, I think I know what you mean. After my cancer, I had to come back to the beach to heal. It was just calling me. I needed the beach more than anything, I thought. Okay, so the ocean makes us happy. There are people that go surfing all the time, but are they all really happy people too? I think you and I are happy because of the gospel, and therefore, when we have time to think and feel peaceful around the ocean it is because we are living right. If we were not living the gospel of Jesus Christ, I am not so sure we would be this happy at the ocean."

Matt replied, "Yes. The gospel does have a lot to do with my happiness—you are right. I just love surfing though, and to give that up for two years would be difficult. Why can't I just go to some island and surf everyday and teach the people when I am out there surfing, and then at night, teach them in their homes? That would be ideal. I think that would be the perfect mission for me."

I don't remember what I said after that, but later he did serve a mission in Washington DC and gave up surfing for two years. I wrote him on his mission, and I loved getting his letters. He was a great missionary.

Chapter 33

False hope

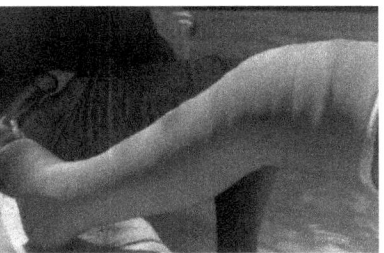

My full length hot pink glow in the dark cast

Karen and I

About the same time I broke my leg, Karen, my good friend whom I met in Park City, had just gotten back from Japan where she was teaching English. So she planned to come help take care of me. When she was there staying with me at the Santos's house, the Rodney King L. A. riots broke out and some of it was not that far from where we were staying In Long Beach.

I wrote in my journal the following.

Dear Journal,

Karen and I watched the news about the Rodney King riots happening around us but mostly in LA. It was kind of scary because it was like a battlefield out there. I am still on disability and I am enjoying having Karen to hang out with. I am glad we did not have to pick Karen up at LAX this week, or we would have been even closer to the riots. We are just staying safe inside. It happened because of the Rodney King trial. It is awful. People are burning down buildings, looting stores, killing people, and shooting at nothing. And actually some of it was happening 5 miles away. It sounds worse than it was because I did not see it in person but watched it all on the news. The news stations covered the violence for almost 48 hours before giving it a rest. It was sad, but the happy part of it all was it really made people—the good people pull together to help each other clean up the mess. There was a drive at work for a Homeless shelter in LA. I was in charge of bringing the collected items to the shelter. I met the woman, a pastor, who ran the mission, and she was a very beautiful person. She was so filled with love, and joy I saw it in her eyes. They shined. When I meet people like her, I have hope for the world.

Lately, I have been dating some. I went out with a guy, Brendon, that a friend set me up with. On our first date, we went skiing. That was before I went to Utah to ski and broke my leg. Brendon had been married before, and he was now visiting me at the Santos's house quite a bit after I broke my leg. He was really going all out to make sure I was being taken care of. He even loaned me his automatic drive car since mine was stick, so I could drive once my half cast was on.

Karen and I drove with him to Utah, for a short trip, while I was still on disability because he had to go to a family member's graduation, and I went to take Karen home and see my family.

I was starting to feel like Brendon liked me a lot. He acted like he did, so I started to really like him back too. Then, when we came home, he stopped calling me as often, and when I called him he said he was leaving to move up

North and marry some girl he had met. He had mentioned her once before but said he was not even interested in her. It was strange. I felt kind of crushed, but I knew it was for the best. He did help me with my broken leg situation, so it was nice for a while to have some male friendship, or whatever it was. I was very confused about what had happened at the end, and I never had the chance to find out.

Karen told me a saying that seemed to apply to Brendon when I felt crushed when he suddenly did not like me anymore. She said, there is a saying; "If you loan someone 5 dollars, and then you never see them again, it was worth the 5 dollars." I had been vulnerable, and I had given him my friendship and love which was worth more than 5 dollars. Then he was gone, so I decided I was the lucky one.

Chapter 34

Near death

I had moved up to Irvine right before I broke my leg skiing. I moved in with a friend from the single's ward. Living in Irvine was very good for me. I was meeting new single friends and seeing some old friends too. I really liked where I lived including the beaches down south. One time, I even went to the beach with my cast still on and put a plastic bag over it to go into the waves. Because it did not work very well, I had to go get a new cast. The doctor was not pleased. I couldn't wait to finally get my cast off. It has been almost 6 months.

The only good thing about my cast was that I could park in Handicapped parking, so when we all went to the beach, we could park very close to the curb at Corona Del Mar and Laguna Beach where parking is normally hard to find. When I'd finally did get my cast off, my leg was skinny and white. The rest of my body was very tan from summer beach trips.

I did not have long to get my cast off, and I couldn't wait! The week my cast was off, I went on a river run working as the cook on the Killer Kern River located in central

California. I was taking my room-mate's place. It was her brother's river running company. She usually went to help, but she couldn't go, so I was taking her place. I was so excited.

While on the river, our raft got stuck, and we had to hop the rocks to get to the side. My leg was still weak, and I made a very novice decision by trying to grab my ore from the rapids as it went by me, while standing on a rock, and the force of the water pulled me right into Level 3 rapids.

Unfortunately, my life jacket was not tight enough to keep my nose and mouth above water. I knew that I was suppose to lay back and then go feet first while on my back, but the water was flipping me whatever way it wanted me to go. I took in so much water, and I was choking and coughing and taking in even more water. Just as I started to think I might die, I began to feel dizzy like I would pass out, and then the rapids ended. The group was yelling for me on the river bank. Fortunately, I got up and made it to the side safely.

Chapter 35

Care-free

While living in Irvine, I enjoyed my roommates. Even though I attended the single's ward activities, I went to the family ward where I served as the nursery leader. I loved playing with the nursery kids every Sunday and preparing the lessons for them. I had heard from my friends at my old job at the RTC in Utah that little Sean's adoption had failed. I was thinking to myself that I need to contact him and let him know that I was thinking about him.

I wrote in my journal the following.

Dear Journal,

Life is excellent! Today I was set apart as the Nursery leader. In the setting apart, great things were said in reference to the little boy Sean from my job at the children's RTC who I have been trying to help since his adoption placement did not work out. I have been spending time with him when I am in Utah and also calling him. I have thought about adopting him, but I think he needs both a mom and a dad. He will be able to be put up for adoption again soon, when he is ready. In the blessing, I was told that many great things would happen for Sean, even Miracles. The blessing also told me to prioritize my life and that, as I made good decisions in my life, blessings would come. I love life. Although there are no men in my life right now, life is still fun. I am going waterskiing this weekend, last weekend rock climbing, and yesterday I enjoyed the beach. I guess my priorities are still high on the fun side. Maybe this is the side of life where I need to prioritize more. Oh well, I better go to bed.

    Sean was so cute on the phone last time I talked to him. I hope he can be adopted, but I wish I could meet a man, and together, we could adopt him. I really want to help him. We have a bond, so I know I will be able to help him some way.

Goodnight, Nancy

    Living in Irvine had been good for my social life. I met many friends there. Two of my friends and I rented a red convertible and took a road trip to San Francisco along the coast. I visited Carol Harvey Stewart again. She had moved up in that area because Kevin, her husband, was going to chiropractic school up there. She was very happy, and they had 2 girls now. It was another great road trip.

While living in our house in Irvine, I continued painting. I had many other things to keep my life balanced including exercise, church dances, parties and frequent trips to Utah. Each time I went to Utah, I spent more time with little Sean as well.

Matt was now on his mission in Washington DC, and I received a letter from him.

Hey Nancy,

I worry that you are being too social!!!! You are such a teenager, always partying. Off to Utah skiing, and then the next thing you know, you're hanging off a cliff or a rock somewhere, then, you're off in the middle of the ocean watching huge creatures jumping out of the water. You are awesome.

Guess where I'm at??? I am serving in inner city DC.

Guess who I have the privilege of serving?

THE AFRICANS!!!! I am in the African program, and it is truly the best! The African people are so spiritual. They "Put God First."

I really liked your letter. I can tell that you were feeling really spiritual and good that morning. My testimony grows daily. Know there is a missionary in DC that cares about you a lot.

        Elder Wong

        Your Eternal Bud!

Chapter 35

Signs of infertility

I was offered a job in Fullerton, closer to where I am now living in Irvine. After I started my new job in Fullerton, I decided to go to a doctor about my hormones because of the hot flashes and mood swings that I was having.

Dear Journal,   8/7/93

Today I went to see a new doctor while using my new insurance at my new job. He is an OBGYN because it has been 6 months since I had a period. I thought my periods were going to come back. They were starting to get more regular, or at least I was starting to have them again after chemo, but now it has been 6 months! I was told by this doctor that I might be going into an early menopause and that my ovaries might be shutting down. He is going to do a blood test to see if I have much estrogen in me. I cried in the doctor's office today, but I feel torn because of what my patriarchal blessing says," It shall not be exceedingly difficult for you to bring children into the world." So I believe this is true, and somehow I will have children. It is just all very confusing right now, but it feels good to say I will have children. I guess I should just fast and pray.

The doctor also mentioned that if I choose to get pregnant, there is a risk that my cancer will come back due to the fact that estrogen levels increase so much during pregnancy. I feel somewhat sad and scared, but I also know I can just trust in my Savior more. I just wish life was easier right now. Why can't anything be simple? Maybe someday I'll feel better about this. Hopefully I will soon. Tomorrow I am going to the temple. That always helps me.

About 4 months later I wrote in my journal again on November 10. 1993

Dear Journal,

I'm feeling a lot better. Last September I finally had a period, so it was 7 months without a period and my moods have now improved a lot. Unfortunately, I have not had another one for 2 months now. The one I did have, in September, was a very normal one lasting 5 days with bloating and cramps too. My body felt great afterwards. It made me feel like my body was working after all!

I also felt better because I quit my stressful job in Fullerton. The money was great, but my bosses were crazy, and I am now moving back to Utah too. It just seems right, even though now I am having doubts. Not really, though because I love my family, especially my nieces and nephews, and I need to be around them.

Also, I can spend more time with little Sean, Sarah and her family too. It is just time to leave California. Also I am between jobs. Hopefully I will have one in February, I think, I hope I do.

As I was saying, I'm between jobs, so I decided to take this opportunity to go to Europe. Yes, I did say Europe! (You did read this right.) Can you believe me driving around Europe for 25 days? I'm very excited, but I also feel this is what I am supposed to do. Maybe it's like a mission. Maybe there is a purpose for this trip besides seeing Europe! I hope so because I feel stressed sometimes about spending the money. Oh, we are going cheap for Europe from the plane ticket, only 450 dollars, to all our plans being at the lowest cost. Amy Hanson, my friend from my BYU days, and now she and I both live in Irvine, is going with me to Europe. She was a travel agent, and she got us the deal. Then we will do the backpack and youth hostel thing in Europe. We will stay with friends too. Then in England, we will stay in a Bed and Breakfast using Steve Rick's "Europe through the Back Door" guide, and we'll stay with my two mission friends near Manchester. It will be so much fun! I will write more at a later time.

I have to get up early and pack my car because I am driving to Utah tomorrow for an interview. I will take some of my stuff on this trip too. I am a little nervous for this interview, but I should not be. I have an excellent recommendation from my friends Ellen and James (former co-workers in Utah). I feel like everything will just keep falling into place, just like it has been. It always does that when it is a right decision. It is all falling into place. I need to have faith. I am learning to trust more in my Heavenly Father. This is all for now.

Love Nancy

Europe trip was perfect. We saw good friends, wonderful art, beautiful ancient buildings, castles, and I met my first cousin fifteen generations removed in the towns of Trubach and Seelbach near Siegen, Germany where some of my ancestors came from. I stood in a fifteenth century schoolhouse where my ancestors went to school. I also gathered so many names to add to my family tree. There are more than a 100 new names. I also drove in some towns in Graubünden, Switzerland, where many of my ancestors came from. I felt their influence as I tried to gather their information.

Amy and I eating out in The Hague

Me at St. Mark's Square Venice, Italy

On April 4th 1994 I wrote in my journal the following.

Dear Journal,

It has been a long time. I went to Europe last December, and I did keep a separate journal of some of my experiences in Europe. I am now living in Salt Lake City with my parents and working for Salt Lake County as a Recreational Therapist and Deer Valley ski resort in child care. I get a free ski pass there!

Today I heard from my doctor. He said that I am in menopause. I am feeling very upset and sad. I can't stop crying. I have had a lot of sadness but some happiness too. Conference weekend and Easter were this past weekend. It is always so comforting to listen to the LDS General Conference. Some good news, I have Sean with me two times a week now, so I guess he is doing better overall.

I don't understand this about being in menopause because it says in my patriarchal blessing, "It shall not be exceedingly difficult for me to bring children into the world." I believe, or at least part of me believes, this means I will have children in this life even more than one because logically (but I know logic does not really work when talking about spiritual matters), why would it say it like this?

"It will not be exceedingly difficult for you to bring children into the world."

Why couldn't it say, "You will bring children into the world?" But it does not say this. It says, "It won't be exceedingly difficult..." maybe because the doctor will tell me it will be exceedingly difficult.

I believe the words of my blessing. I will have the faith to have those children. Then part of me thinks that maybe it is not going to happen in this life. I believe that is possible. Anyways, I am sorry I have not written much. I have been very moody, had hot flashes, confused thinking, and my hormones are all messed up. Today the 2nd FSH test is also very high in the last 8 months, meaning my estrogen is depleting quickly. Because of my breast cancer, I can't take estrogen to try to get it back. That is according to some doctors, but some studies show it is really okay for me. Who knows? All I know, is I want a baby someday soon. I wish. Bye for now.

Love, Nancy

Chapter 36

Kiss ovaries goodby?

After I had moved back to Utah, I had a terrible visit with an OBGYN in Utah. I was asking simple questions about if my body could still get pregnant, when his response to my questions about if I could have children was, "Honey you got to face it. You just got to kiss your ovaries goodbye."

I thought to myself, "I guess he got an F in bedside manner class when he was in medical school." I could not stop crying.

All my life, I knew that I wanted to have children, and I imagined myself having at least 10 kids or more. It just seemed like what I would do. And now, someone was telling me I might have no children, and I really believed I would have children. What a shock! I was not willing to believe this man.

Later, Amy, my friend from Park City, referred me to my new, Doctor. She was so much better. I remember she would test my FSH levels and tell me that it was very high, meaning my estrogen was very low. She explained that the FSH was high because it was trying to stimulate the ovaries to produce more estrogen. My cancer was estrogen receptor positive, meaning the cancers cells fed off of my abundance of estrogen. Hence, that is how my original cancerous lump grew.

Ironically, during the time my cancer was growing inside me, it was the excessive estrogen being produced by my ovaries that would have helped me have a baby in the future, but it then became the very thing that caused my cancer. So, the estrogen that would have allowed me to have babies has now taken that chance away from me by feeding the cancer cells instead, which in turn, required me to have chemotherapy. Now they say it took away any opportunity to get pregnant! Not cool!

I loved my new doctor because she answered all my questions and did not dwell on the negatives. She would also tell me stories of women who were in menopause, when out of the blue somehow, became pregnant while on a cruise with their husband. She gave me hope. I needed that. Now finding my husband became even more important to me. My biological clock was ticking very fast.

Chapter 37

Fostering a child

Time continued on, as it always does. Eventually I was hired at the Utah State Hospital in Provo, Utah, to work on the girl's adolescent unit. I loved working there. It felt like I was a Young women's leader at church, some of the time.

I moved into an apartment with roommates; Sean came some weekends. His therapist asked me if I was interested in being his foster mom because he had not been adopted, and he was now age 12 years old. He needed this to avoid growing up while being institutionalized most of his growing up years. I was his only hope. It became crucial to get him out and into a home environment and then to have experience with family life and even opportunities to learn to bond with others.

I became a single mom on August 1, 1995. I moved into a duplex and tried my best to help Sean learn to bond. I was active in all aspect of Sean's life from IEP school meetings, daily contact with his SPED teacher, scouting at church, Junior Jazz basketball, and in his therapies as well. I hired an excellent child care nanny for when I was at work, and then again when I took a trip to China for 2 weeks with friends to go to the Hong Kong Temple dedication.

My social life was improving too. I was even having time to date a little here and there. The RTC staff was always there for additional support (Respite care) for both me and Sean, especially when he pushed the limits too far with his lying and stealing tactics.

Before I became Sean's fulltime foster mom, I took him on several vacations with friends and then again while he lived with me. We went twice to California, once to Zion and Bryce National Parks, and once to Jackson Hole, Wyoming on a River run with the National Ability Center. We also took frequent visits to see little Sarah's family for the day or weekend.

One day, I wrote in my journal after taking Sean to time-out at the residential treatment center at the RTC, the following.

Dear Journal, 10/1/95

It is conference weekend; I listened to most of the conference but not the last session because I had to take Sean back to the RTC to sit out for some time-out. He has been very rude and disobedient toward me for the last few days, so I just felt like I did not deserve this behavior. It seems that he has come to love my anger at him. Usually I get angry, just give consequences, and then it is over. I got tired of him trying to pull me into his anger and being pulled into this game he is playing with me. I try to ignore the stuff that I can, but the overt disobedience I can't ignore. Too much arguing and passive aggressiveness got to me, and I lost it. I took him to the RTC for a time out. I hopefully can pick him up tonight if he has not ruined his time there. I am not sure I could handle him if he has not changed at least a little bit. It is so hard. I have cried a lot, and so has he. I am not giving up on him yet, but I am glad I have respite care in place. I hope he will be better after seeing the reality and difference between home life and institutional life. I just called the RTC, and they said, "All he has said is, I want to go home." He is sitting in time-out, and he has written about 10 things he has done wrong. He says he does not know why he is pushing me away. I guess with all his confusion this could be true. I will go get him.

I am glad that I have a social life now because it is really helping me to have fun when times get tough. I went out with friends from my mission and ate Chinese food, and I have been dating some too. That's all for now.

Nancy

Since my breast cancer, about six years ago, I had many mammograms and they were all were negative. Now, on January 15th 1996, I wrote the following in an excerpt in my journal.

Dear Journal,

….. Now the thing I dread to mention was that my mammogram that I did at the end of December has a swollen node showing up. It could be caused by just being sick with some infection that caused it to swell. It is under my left arm this time. The doctors did a needle aspiration, and the results will be back on Tuesday. Tomorrow is Tuesday. The truth is I am scared! I am trying to believe it is nothing, but I am scared. I am not afraid to die. Opps! I almost wrote, "I am not afraid to die. I can live with that." (I just made myself laugh). The part I don't want to go through is losing a breast or going through chemotherapy. I was told you cannot radiate a breast twice, so this time I would have to get a mastectomy. And chemo would be horrible again too.

Plus, now I have Sean, and it would be more difficult with him. Who knows? It is best not to stress about until I know for sure. So that is what I am trying to do. I also feel like I need to prepare for whatever it is. I don't mean dying. I mean be emotionally prepared to accept it if it is cancer. There, I said that awful word. I have mixed feelings about that word because cancer, in a way, is one of my friends because it taught me so much about life. It changed me to be somebody I love. ME. It taught me to be more Christ-centered than I have ever felt or lived before. I am not saying that I am perfect because I am not at all. I am just more honest with who I am than I was before, and it feels good to accept yourself as you are. If I have to live through this again then this time I WILL lean on my Savior much more and will not let myself be afraid of anything. I will completely put fear away and fight with all I have to love the best I can. I will love others the best I can because that is all Heavenly

Father and Christ expect from us. If I can do that, I will be completely prepared for whatever work Heavenly Father and Christ need me to do. If that means to be a great mom for Sean, with His help, I can do it! If that means never having children of my own that come from my eggs, then I can do that. If that means never marrying, I can do that too. In fact, I can do anything with His help; I can even be cured of cancer the 2nd time around. Maybe I don't even have it! Who knows until tomorrow? Life will be good no matter what happens. It already is good. I have friends who love me lots. I have family that is always there for me and the gospel, the scriptures that I need to read more often, the temple, my ancestors, and last but not least, I have Sean, as difficult as he is, I do love him. I just hope he will be able to learn the things he needs to learn. I do love him, and Christ loves him, so together, we can help him. Well that's all for now.

Love Nancy

PS I am going to China to the Hong Kong temple dedication in the end of May.

The next day I wrote January 16th 1996

Dear Journal,

The tests are negative for cancer. He said to find the lump and check it daily, and if it starts to change and get bigger, then I will have to have it taken out and biopsied. I am so happy. Thank you Heavenly Father for my life. Yeah! And I am thankful for my BREASTS. I love them and I don't want to lose them.

Thanks Nancy

PS I have got to go to work. Sean is now going to public school, and he starts tomorrow. He has moved on from the Wasatch Mental Health Day Treatment School he was attending to public school.

That year, I was able to do many good things for Sean. During that year, Sean took Private Ski lessons at National Ability center (Formally Park City Handicapped Sports Center) where I used to work. I tried to give him a fun and normal life. We spent holidays with family, and my family was very supportive of him.

Unfortunately, though in the spring, Sean did push the limits too far. He was arrested at school for stealing books at the book fair, and he gave away the stolen items to whomever he felt like giving it to making difficult to get back the stolen goods.

The book fair company pressed charges, so he was put on probation, and later, he eventually went back to a group home in his home state where he was originally from. It was my understanding that he could earn his way back into my home after he worked more on his issues of stealing.

I soon learned that the caseworker for Sean lied to us. She never had any intentions of having him come back ever. The state was planning to phase out all Interstate Compact contracts and only allow them for permanent adoptions. Since I had not adopted Sean, he could not come back. At first, I had some contact with Sean, and I told him he could come back after he worked on his stealing issues and when he was ready—because that is what I had been told. After we spoke, he started acting out at the group home, so they cut off contact with me. I heard he was even doing worse after that.

His caseworker was a joke. She had an incredibly large caseload, as most caseworkers do, but she was also a very busy real estate agent, and she had a private adoption counseling practice. It was clear to me that she did not see Sean like she claimed she did, and she was probably not making the required visits in her caseload. I found out she would write up reports about Sean without any contact or speaking to anyone about him. It was obvious to me she cared about money, not kids. I felt betrayed by those who I thought cared about Sean. I was now struggling with my own guilt of sending him there. I had heard they now had Sean heavily medicated to deal with his behaviors.

Chapter 38

Promised blessings

Shortly after this time, my great aunt on my mom's side was diagnosed with breast cancer. When I was diagnosed, no one in my family on either side ever had it. My Aunt Ellen was living in San Marcos, California, and I took another road trip to California with a friend and neighbor in my family ward, and we visited her. She made it through her treatments. She was in her 80's, and she lived quite a few years after that.

On September 10th I wrote in my journal:

Dear Journal,

….. Also, I must tell you that the swollen lymph node from my (1996) mammogram has gotten bigger, so Sept 20th they will be taking it out to make sure it is not cancer. I'm scared, but I know I can handle whatever cancer brings. I really feel blessed. I really believe that most people that have gone through this much stress would be crazy, and I am amazed I am not completely crazy by now!

I also have been going out on a few dates, but I am not sure if I am in a good situation to have a relationship right now. Maybe later I can. He is a good friend, I think.

Love,

Nancy

My life slowed down. No more Europe or China trips, and being a single parent was over. I had traveled so much in the last year. There was Europe for 28 days and China for 2 weeks. Then I went to Florida for 1 week for a Recreational Therapy conference, and I, of course, turned that trip into a vacation too, and I met up with my old roommate, April, and we went to the beach and sightseeing. We went for a sunrise swim in the Atlantic and sunset swim in the Gulf all in the same day.

Now, with my job responsibilities planning camp trips and river runs for the girls finally slowing down, I was focused more on myself. I was finishing up a quick trip to Arizona to see Matt get married before I had surgery.

I flew to Arizona to go to the temple wedding in Mesa. I stayed at a friend's house; I was waiting for my ride to the temple, but she did not come. I did not have her phone number. I was so sad that I was going to not make it to Matt's wedding. I began to pray hard, and as I prayed, I prayed for my upcoming surgery too. I was feeling like I probably had cancer again. That day, I poured my heart out in my friend's condo. I felt inspired to get a paper and pencil, and I began to write. I wrote several sentences down which were answers to my prayer. One of the sentences I wrote stated, "You will meet your husband in the near future."

After the wedding (which I did miss) and while I was back home in Provo, I was wondering about this "meeting my husband in the near future" as I waited for the upcoming surgery.

Before the surgery, I was talking to my Bishop about my trials, and he gave me a blessing. I wrote about it in my journal.

Dear Journal,

Today, I received a beautiful blessing from my Bishop. Through the priesthood power he told me I needed to have faith and that through Christ, there would be miracles performed through my faith. He blessed me with patience in my afflictions, with peace, spiritual strength, and a strong mind. He also told me, speaking about Sean, that I would be able to handle these trials in my life and eventually witness miracles. He also counseled me to stay close to my Heavenly Father and Christ. He also told me that the Lord was pleased with the things that I was doing in my life and because I was staying faithful. It felt good to know the Lord had that much confidence in my abilities. He also told me to prioritize my life. (This has been said in many blessings in my life.) I will do this! He also told me to hold onto my strength and that I would be an example of strength for others. He told me there was an important reason why I needed to go through these trials and this reason would be made known to me at a later time. He counseled me to walk with my Savior—that he would be there with me always—and to rely and lean on Him. I loved this blessing. It gave me the spiritual strength I needed. I am leaving on a 4 day camp trip with work, and I will get home the day before the surgery.

Nancy

The night before the surgery, my dad gave me another blessing, and it said all the same things that my bishop's blessing said. My surgery went as scheduled, and my surgeon was the same surgeon as last time. After the surgery, he called that very night to tell me, "So far the frozen biopsy does not look at all like cancer." I was so happy because with all the counsel in my blessing about my trials, I was really thinking it would be cancer. Later, the tests confirmed it was not cancer, and the lymph node was benign. I was so happy!

During this time, Sean's caseworker was still not letting me or anyone from Utah have contact with Sean. I missed him, and I really believed they were hurting him; I was worried for Sean.

I pushed hard and met with people over the caseworker's head, and I finally was able to come and visit with him over Christmas. He had massively regressed and was so different. They also had him on so much medication; I felt sorry for him. I tried to keep in contact, but they still did not allow him visits and phone calls. He continued to go downhill.

I found out later that his house parents were thinking of adopting him, but they changed their minds and did not adopt him either. Now I was not in any position to take him into my home, especially when he had regressed so much.

He needed 24 hour supervision now, and I could not offer that. I had to let go and move on with my life.

I focused on the things I could control myself, my job, and tried to do my best at both. I had many friends and was training BYU Recreational therapy students on their Internships as part of my job. All of this kept me busy. I was sad, and I missed Sean.

Chapter 39

Meeting my husband!

It was February 1997—about 4 months since I was told that I would meet, in the near future, my husband. I was dating more; one night, my friend and I decided to plan a dinner party, but we wanted to find some new guys to invite. While going to a single ward's activity that involved playing Lazar tag, we met my future husband and he gave us his phone number. He called us later. We invited him to a dinner party at my friend's new condo.

The night of the dinner party, my friend was getting ready for the party upstairs, and I was cooking with my left arm because a few days before I'd broke my arm while trying snowboarding for the first time. Right at the exact time that the dinner party was to start, the door bell rang. I answered it since my friend was upstairs getting ready. He was standing in the doorway holding a gallon of cranberry juice. He looked cute standing there. I thought to myself, "Cranberry juice? That's what old people drink."

"Hi, you're right on time." I said. "Come in. I am cooking in the kitchen, you can help me." He followed me into the kitchen. He looked at my arm all wrapped up and swollen, he did not say anything. "I said, "I broke my arm two days ago snowboarding—my right arm, so this is kind of hard to make dinner. You can help make the salad." I gave him the lettuce and everything else for the salad. I remember he chopped everything so exact and perfect. He did it much better than I would have done. Then he was helping me boil the pasta and vegetables for our Mediterranean pasta shrimp main dish.

I was impressed with him and immediately felt attracted to him. After the meal, we all sat down in the living room. There were about 12 people there so there were not enough seats for everyone. He sat on the couch, and I went over and sat right in front of him using his legs against the couch as a back rest. He took notice of my seating placement and told me later that he liked how I did that. I guess I was subconsciously saying, this is my guy stay away (to the other women there).

Before he left, he asked if he could meet us at church the next day at the Monument Park single's Ward. None of us were in the ward, but all were planning to attend the next day. He showed up and sat next to me in church. We sat close and talked before and after church.

We were still getting to know each other, and I think I asked him, "What is the coolest thing you have ever done? He said, "I dove off a submarine into the Bermuda triangle." I had never met anyone who had done that before. I could not even top that. I was intrigued. I sat closer to him. After church he drove me to a friend's house for a baby shower for my California roommate, April. Her mother in law had it on a Sunday so some relatives could be there. I was glad he could help because I could not drive myself with my broken arm.

Later, he told me he was going to the temple that week. I asked him if I could go with him. He said "Yes, I'll pick you up." We went to a temple session; it was nice. A few weeks later he told me that he knew he was going to marry me after spending time in the temple together. He said he just felt it and it was inspiration from above.

Later he told me about his pending divorce and that would be final any day. I told him I could not see him again until it was final. A few days later, he brought proof of his divorce papers, and we started dating. Within a few weeks, he asked me to marry him. I was nervous, but it was so different than any other time I had been asked before. He gave me the proposal in a gold frame and he gave me a very nice sized diamond ring all wrapped up. It was so fast. I was speechless. Was this the guy I was promised in my patriarchal blessing? The proposal was as follows and was given to me with 3 red roses and 2 white roses.

Nancy

The Circle of Eternal Love.

(As represented by five roses)

(Red rose #1) is the love of life as characterized by the motto

"To Be One and To Have Fun"

(Red Rose #2) is the love of a lion: productivity and leadership in service to God to each other and in service to fellowman.

(Red Rose #3) is the love of a lamb: to be meek, lowly in heart, gentle, temperant, tolerant, and patient toward each other through all of the hills and the valleys of life. Also to be a like a child always submissive to Heavenly Father's will.

(White Rose #1) Is the love from our dear brother Jesus Christ and His desire for us to love without condition, to have charity, to sacrifice, and to always love with pure hearts and oneness with each other and oneness with God.

(White rose #2)... represents my love for you.

Love, Bart

I was so amazed and touched by the message in his proposal. Later, when I was alone, I knew he was the man I had been waiting for. How could he get any more perfect than to write a motto that says, *"To Be One and Have Fun."* After waiting for so long for him, sometimes when thinking about this, I would hyperventilate and think is this really happening? I actually had to breathe in a bag to calm down. It was so exciting to have this happening, even if it was very late at age 40.

Bart and I the day we were
sealed in the Jordan River temple.

Me skiing at work before I broke my arm snowboarding

Chapter 40

Honeymoon

We were married and sealed in the Jordan River temple with all our family and friends present. Joe and Helen Santos were there too.

We went on an awesome two week honeymoon by taking our brand new jeep wrangler and camping on the beach along the coast from Canada to Mexico. We stayed the first night at the Homestead in Midway, Utah, so we did not camp that night. The next night, we camped by the Snake River in Idaho. We then camped in the mountains in Oregon; next on Vancouver Island, and then back down the coast until eventually to San Felipe, Mexico. We camped on the beach there too.

Some funny things that happened included being pulled over in Washington and making Bart 'walk the line'—I guess we were drunk with love? We both don't drink, so it was funny. We were also searched for drugs at the border in Canada. Then in Mexico, in the middle of nowhere (the Baja), we were pulled over and harassed by the Mexican military and searched again. They took the cowboy hat that

Bart bought in Mendocino, California. They also took my scriptures but then gave it all back.

On our way back to Utah we had another wedding reception at Jennifer's house in California. It was wonderful to see all the good people in California that could not make it to the Utah reception at Carla's house. Carol drove all the way down by herself from Central California to come to our reception. It was so wonderful to see her and have her meet Bart.

Carol Harvey Stewart, me, and one of her girls

Chapter 41

Step-motherhood

After the celebrations, my life had changed dramatically. I was married and now was a step-mom of six children. The children lived with their mother, in the beginning mostly, but through the years one by one five out of the six children lived with us at different times. In the beginning we saw them all, frequently, and we were a part of their lives in any way we could be.

Sean had a new caseworker and he was still struggling. His new caseworker gave permission for him to come and live with us with the hope that we could eventually adopt him. When Sean came he was on so much medication and in very poor health. He could barely walk a half block. We wanted to adopt him and because he was older at 15 years old, we wanted him to be part of the decision to adopt.

Sean still had a problem with lying and stealing. While he lived with us, we told him that if he wanted to be adopted, he had to work for this. He also continued to see his old Utah therapist when needed or wanted to.

My husband Bart and I had consequences in place for Sean, and we tried to structure his time productively. Part of his program was that he was to walk a 1/2 mile, at first, for any lie or theft we caught him in. He usually liked to get caught because he was always testing us out and pushing us away when he felt too close. He was soon walking 5 or more miles a day and was getting fit and even getting good grades. My husband Bart would sit down with him as well as with Bart's oldest son (who also lived with us) and structure them in getting their homework done. Boys need fathers. I saw that with my own step-sons and with Sean. They do their best when they have a good relationship with their dad.

Sean lasted about 1 year before he was arrested for felony theft of computers in our community. He went back to the group home. This time they never took away any contact and contact with us was encouraged. I think they were amazed how much Sean's health improved in body and mind. Too bad the obsessive lying and stealing couldn't be dealt with as easily. Sean would tell me later on the phone that he has great memories of his long walks through the country side in Utah where we lived, and that he is proud of the grades he accomplished while he lived with us.

Chapter 42

A new beginning & desires for children

I was working and thinking about getting a master's degree too, but most of all, I was still wishing for a baby. While taking a poetry class at the University of Utah, after 2 years of being married, I wrote this poem about my life's adjustment to being married.

Ode to My Marriage

It was a new beginning- from single life to now being a wife, and step mom. Me, now a new bride Emerging into a life with something old, new, borrowed, and blue.

Leaves of the past falling slowly, suspended in time like my thoughts of anticipation, lingering, like sparks from a bonfire from the night before.

A new beginning, relished with stored-up remembrance of forty years of single life.

A new beginning attached with a paste made from a love of life. A new beginning, stretching my arms, reaching with my insides, yearning for dreams yet to come, commenced in childhood and cherished into adulthood. Some of those childhood dreams now have become reality.

There are piled-up leaves, into small mountains of fun, jumping, diving, and crunching under tiny feet.

There are snowflakes, icy days and roaring fires in the fireplace at night, and snowboarding under the moonlight while taking on the black diamonds.

Now springtime has come, excited, rush for Easter eggs.

Searching for the prize!

And summertime! Oh, summertime. The long days are like years, being lazy in the heat of noon, swimming, or being barefoot and cooled down only by the hose in the front yard, with fresh-cut grass.

Now there are tiny sweaty foreheads, sugary popsicles with sticky fingers. Now, I buy those popsicles. And I clean those sticky fingers, rake those leaves, hide those eggs before the hunt, and I wipe those sweaty foreheads.

And swim with the fish, give swim lessons and blow bubbles till I drop! Feed the dog, talk to the teen, do dishes, laundry, bubble-baths for a 3-year old. Wash hair, not mine. Bake birthday cakes and take pictures with Mickey Mouse.

The Europe and China trips are gone, as are the Friday night dates and dancing into the night.

No more just dreaming who will be the man I'll spend forever with. It's almost been two years now, and I'm beginning to be assimilated into a new beginning, married to a man with six children and one foster son.

Friday night, there is always a date. So what if it ends by falling asleep in front of the TV watching a Jazz game.

And the stored-up memories of forty years of single life are only fleeting moments of times gone by.

This is real- it is love- watching him working
hard in the yard or playing with a child. This
is lasting. This is forever.

Nancy K. Bowen

In the first year we were married, Bart's oldest son lived with us and Sean our foster son had been with us for about a year. After about a year and a half, they both were gone. It was quiet. I was still wishing and hoping to get pregnant by some miracle.

The first year I was married, I was being set apart to be a counselor in the Relief Society, the Woman's organization of the church. The Bishop was setting me apart as a counselor in the presidency by the laying on of hands. In the blessing he stopped talking about the calling, there was a long pause, and then he said, "Nancy, your Heavenly Father wants you to know that he is aware of your desire for children. He wants you to know that your desire for children will be granted, but for now He wants you to focus on the children that you do have now." He then went on with the setting apart for my new calling. After the setting apart, the bishop asked my husband if I had difficulty having children. The bishop told him that he had felt strongly to tell me this while he was setting me apart, and he had not known why.

After this, I tried to do as my Heavenly Father said and focus on my step children, foster son, and any other children that I might be able to have some positive influence on that came my way.

Chapter 43

Battling infertility

I still could not let go of my desire for children. On one Mother's day, I had this experience:

My Mother's Day Miracle

It was Mother's day, and I had almost been married for 2 years on June 6th. I had been thinking a lot about having a baby and wishing that I could get pregnant. The week before Mother's day, I passed by a sign near the hospital where I worked that announced an upcoming lecture on the latest research on infertility. This, and the fact that it was almost Mother's day, pushed my desire to have children first and foremost into my mind.

It had been about ten years since I had experienced breast cancer, at age 32. Because of having treatments, my body was thrown into an early peri-menopausal state. Some doctors believed that I would never have children. Nevertheless, I still had not given up hope due to the fact that my patriarchal blessing seemed to state I would have children.

All week long I had been thinking about what it would be like to have this joy of Motherhood. To rock and nurse a baby that I had carried for 9 months was my forever and not forgotten, longing wish. Usually around Mother's day, I would try to forget my lack of baby in my life. Instead I'd think about my own Mother and how grateful I was for all that she taught me. It seemed that this year was different. I was fighting a depression about my inability to have children. I felt alone.

Even though I had a wonderful marriage with a man who honored his priesthood and was supportive of me in all my endeavors, including recently being a wonderful father for 11 months to a very troubled teenage foster son. I still felt alone. Maybe I felt that this way because my husband already had children from his first marriage, six beautiful children who have become a huge part of my life as a stepmother every other weekend and one of his son's that had recently lived with us fulltime for a while for about a year. So I told myself, he doesn't really understand how I feel.

On Mother's day morning, I tried to talk to my husband about my feelings of looking into infertility treatments. We had talked about this before, however, in our past discussions we had both felt like this was not the way for us because we believed that, when the time was right, if the Lord wanted to send us a child, He would do so. This discussion brought on the tears that I had been fighting back all week. I felt so alone and deprived. My husband listened, was kind, and even sympathetic, but I still felt alone. There was a knock on the door while I was crying, but I told my husband not to get it; he continued to try to console me.

We went to church, and the bishop announced that there would be no speakers because the week prior he felt there was insufficient time for testimony bearing so he wanted to have the entire time dedicated to testimony bearing. I was sitting in church reading my book *Glimpses into the Life and Heart of Marjorie Pay Hinckley*. I was reading the chapter on *Motherhood*, and by this time I was really feeling very sorry for myself; I indignantly told my husband while referring to the speakers as they seemed to bask in the joy of their children, "Look at this, this is what they should say over the pulpit on Mother's Day." I read from my book to him, pointing at each word one by one to emphasize my intense feelings I was having about Motherhood. And I quote, *"Have joy in your mothering, whether you are the mother, the aunt, the grandmother, or the next door neighbor. We all have the opportunities to be an influence for good."*

About the same time that I had made this comment to my husband, a woman in the ward that I had spoken with on occasion and been in her home a few times, was bearing her testimony about being a mother. My thoughts, I am ashamed to say, were, this is easy for her to say because she has a beautiful daughter. Her very next words were, "There is a difference in being a mother and mothering." Her comment caught me off guard, and I began to listen. Her comment seemed to be referring to the very sentence I had just pointed out in the book. Suddenly I felt extremely humbled. She went on to say, "There is a sister in the ward that I have been watching. I feel this sister is someone who knows how to mother." She said, "I learn from this sister, my friend, and then she said my name." As she said my name, I suddenly realized how foolish I was being, how negative and selfish. "I do have a choice of how I feel." I told myself. Tears of

288

sorrow came flowing out; but instead of being tears of sorrow, they were tears for the knowledge that I am not alone, and instead, I am part of a wonderful ward family.

One of my sisters knew my heart, and she was able to take away my sorrow by reminding me that I was already a mother in Israel and that I am understood by a loving Heavenly Father more than I could imagine.

After Sacrament meeting, a neighbor came up to me and said that, before church, she had tried to bring a Mother's Day note and cupcakes over to me. She said that she sent it over with her little daughter, but there was no answer at the door. Later, after church, she brought over the Mother's Day note and her homemade cupcakes. In the note she wrote, "Thank you for being an example of motherhood to me as I watched how you have mothered your foster son."

I have had many prayers answered in my life, but I was especially comforted by the way Heavenly Father answered my prayer by teaching me that He knows my thoughts and my heart and that I must never forget to put my faith in Him.

A couple years later, my mom was diagnosed with breast cancer too. She had the mastectomy and chemo too. I know she seemed to have many more problems with the chemo which also caused horrible sores in her mouth, and she was not able to eat much of anything. She had so much pain in her arm and shoulder after the surgery, and it never did get much better. It was hard to see her going through all of this now. I admired her good attitude through it all. I worried that one of my sisters might get it too. My mom got through all her treatments, and her hair grew back nicely.

Chapter 44

Fertility treatment

One day, after we were living in Snowflake, Arizona, working as teachers for about one and half years, and while we had another of my four step son's living with us, I was still thinking and wishing I could get pregnant. We had been married for 13 years by then. While I was reading online, I discovered the latest research about breast cancer survivors and infertility. It now stated that women who were breast cancer survivors did **not** have any more of an increase of reoccurrences of breast cancer after infertility treatments than those that did not get infertility treatments. I told my husband, he consented for us to try having a baby using a donor egg, since my eggs would not work.

After learning this, we met with the doctor. It seemed I would have my baby after all, in my 50's. I went to Utah for fall school break, and while I was there telling my mom the news, I received a phone call from the doctor. The nurse said to me on the phone:

"After the Doctor has reviewed your records, he has decided not to provide treatment to you."

I became defensive and asked.

"Why?"

She said there were too many factors against it.

I said, "Oh I get it. I am a liability, so you don't want a breast cancer survivor. You're afraid of law suits if my cancer came back."

She said, "I am so sorry,"

Before we hung up, I pleaded with her,

"Please don't give up on me."

I went downstairs and pleaded with my Heavenly Father. I cried and cried, "I just want a baby. Why can't I have baby!" I prayed, "Help me get through this. I have never been so sad in my life." I looked around the room for something to give me consolation. I was alone and on my knees. I needed someone's help or inspiration. While on my knees, I randomly pulled a book from the bookcase and read the title, it read, *Mom, Are you there?* I cried even harder. I pulled another book from the shelf, and it read, *For Mother, a Gift of Love.* I threw it on the floor. The phone rang upstairs. I grabbed the phone; it was the nurse again. She then said, "The doctor said that he decided he would take you as a patient." I was elated. I believed with all my heart that my Heavenly Father heard my pleading, and now it was going to happen.

After many doctor appointments, shopping for a donor egg and months of daily shots to prepare my uterus, all while I was working full time teaching first grade on the Navajo reservation, the time came for implantation. My husband was excited too. We knew it was not guaranteed, but we had to try. It was so expensive—so we just paid for one try. We could pay to try again, but we really did not have the money. The day came, and the embryo was inserted.

After implantation, I was told to be very careful, keep even, and not jump around much because it could detach the egg from the uterine wall. The embryo was not even guaranteed to attach to the wall, so I had to stay in bed for the first couple of days to allow this to happen.

After I went back to work, because I worked on the Navajo reservation teaching first grade, I took a very scenic van ride shuttle from the Holbrook school district office to Indian Wells Elementary every day for work. It was a 45 minute drive one way. The reservation roads have some rather large potholes and bumps in the road. In fact, there was one dip in the road that some drivers had actually caught air, landing with a thud. If you were in the back of the van, you could hit your head on the top of the van. Normally, I sat in the back.

I had told a few friends about my infertility treatments, and they were making sure that there was space in front of the van for me so I could sit there. I told whoever the driver was each time we drove that I had a medical procedure done recently and was not allowed medically to be bumped around, so my coworkers slowed down for me on the bumps.

After a week, I went to the Doctor's office in Glendale 3 hours away for a pregnancy test. The results could not be given before we had to leave the site. He would call me in two hours while I was on the road. My cell phone did not work the whole time. Somewhere before Payson, Arizona, the Doctor called and told me the test was positive for pregnancy. I was driving home and felt like my whole life had just begun. My husband was excited, and we both could not believe it was happening. I pulled out an old handwritten letter I had written to my future daughter many years ago before I was even married that I kept in my old Franklin planner that was now just my phonebook. I read it quietly to myself. I did not care if the baby was a boy or a girl, but I read the letter just the same.

It read as follows.

Dear Daughter,

Someday I want to be your mom. I want to be proud of myself when I teach you how to live your life. I want to have wisdom to give you. I want that wisdom to be with me because of how I lived my life. I believe that how I feel about myself will directly affect how good of a mother, how loving of a mother I can be for you. I believe that motherhood is the highest calling of all. I want you to have a Father who loves you like your Heavenly Father loves you. I want you to know that your dad can give you a blessing when you need one. I know that I will be able to provide nothing but the best for you.

Sincerely

With all my love, your mom

I cried thinking about being a mother in the future, and we went home. I called my mom to tell her.

A week later, I went for another pregnancy test locally; it was not positive. It was negative. I thought that it was a mistake. I was told that the pregnancy could have been a false pregnancy or it only lasted a week because the test was positive. I knew I could not try again. I was crushed and told myself that I tried to make it happen, but I knew we did not have the money to do this again.

    I kept the sadness inside, mostly, and went on with my life. It was hard because after this happened there were three pregnant teachers at my school that year. I was happy for them, and I did go to one of their baby showers. I focused on loving my students, and I focused on being a step mom too. My desires for a baby were put away in the back of my heart. After all, I really did know that being a mother and mothering weren't the same thing. I was determined to mother all those that needed to be mothered for all of my life to the best of my ability. This became my resolution. Besides, life is good, isn't it?

Chapter 45

Helping a friend with cancer

Twenty one years later after my breast cancer experience, I had been talking on the phone with my friend, Sandy, a lot. She was my best friend from high school and the first few years of college days. We had many fun, crazy memories together growing up, and we loved to reminisce about the dances and beach parties we went to. Now, she had recently been diagnosed with breast cancer, and I was trying to help her through it.

Earlier, I told her I remembered about 26 or so years ago that I had a dream. At the time, I was not in contact with her. I did not know how to reach her because all her family had moved back to Connecticut. During that time, she had been on my mind.

That night, in my dream, I saw her dad. Her dad had passed away when we were in high school. In the dream, her dad kept saying, "Thank you for taking care of my family." He said this over and over again, and I then woke up. It left a strong impression on me, so I tried to find Sandy but did not find her at that time. Eventually, I did find her through a mutual friend of her sisters and mine.

We had been back in touch for about the 18 years or so. We still had not seen each other for years, but we spoke on the phone and kept in contact with each other by email and more recently by FACEBOOK.

Finally, the year before she had cancer, we all went to our high school reunion together with two other high school friends, Cindy and Zonda. It was great to see them all again. It had been many years, and we all had a fun time together.

Sandy, me, Cindy and Zonda
Class of 75
35 Year Reunion

BFF's Sandy and I age 18

After Sandy had been diagnosed with breast cancer, one night on the phone when we were talking, Sandy told me she was scared because she was feeling so sick from the chemo, and she lived alone. Both her parents were deceased. As I had said, her father died when we were in high school and her mother more recently died in the last 10 years from Alzheimer's. Sandy's oldest sister took care of their mom in her last years. So Sandy had no family living close by. Both of her remaining immediate family members, her sisters lived in Connecticut and were married with children. Sandy had no family close by to help her.

Sandy is incredibly brave, and she was doing her treatments on her own. One night, she told me that she was so sick she was afraid she could die and no one would know until later. I wanted to fly out there, but we did not have the money, so I was trying to console her on the phone just by listening.

Finally I said, "Sandy, if you were going to church and the people in your ward knew you were sick, you would be taken care of. You should not be alone through this. On Sunday, there would have been a sign up for you going around in Relief Society (LDS Church's women's organization) to bring you meals and take you to your Doctor's appointments when you needed help. They would even visit you each day to check up on you and get your needs met." There was a long pause.

Then I said "Do you want me to call your Bishop and tell them about you?" Sandy said, "I have not been to church for 30 years or more." I quickly replied, "That does not matter because you **are** a member of the church of Jesus Christ of Latter day Saints. Anyone there would love to serve you and help you anyway they could. Should I call?" There was another long pause. Finally Sandy said, "Yes, I do want you to call."

I told her I could get the Bishop's number by searching for her ward building at LDS.org by using the "Find a meetinghouse" app and the Bishop's number should be there.

I hung up and quickly found the number. Her Bishop called her that night. The next day, her Relief society president came, and Sandy recognized her because they had known each other through their work. They had both worked in the fashion industry in Los Angeles. The Relief Society president was also single, and she lived very close by to Sandy. They became friends. Many others visited Sandy; meals were brought and blessings were given. I knew that the members would be there for her, and Sandy was amazed that they all came and cared for her.

The treatments that Sandy went through were more difficult than mine were. Her cancer was Her+ and so she would have longer chemo-therapy than me—more intense.

When Sandy was finally done with most of her treatments, we planned a reunion with some of our good friends in Utah.

It was a wonderful day to be with these great women. I feel that I am so blessed to have grown up with Michelle, Diane, Connie, and Sandy. All of our lives turned out so differently, and yet we felt so close because of our common roots and the wonderful friendships that we remarkably still have. Our common bond being that we all grew up in Long Beach and all grew up loving the gospel of Jesus Christ.

Chapter 46

Unexpected death

After I came home from being with my friends, I was thinking about another good friend, Carol Harvey Stewart that I had visited with on so many road trips in California. The last time we had seen each other was when she came to my wedding reception in Long Beach area after Bart and I were married and sealed in Utah at the Jordan River temple in 1997.

Carol and I had spoken on the phone about two years ago after I looked up her phone number on the Internet. I found out she now had six daughters and that she had opened a Yoga and Dance Center. She was living the life I wished I had, even though I loved my life, my husband, and all my wonderful blessings. I was envious because she had six daughters, and she had followed her dreams to open the yoga center too.

When we spoke last, she was so happy that her daughters were going to college. We talked about Costa Rica too because we had both been there lately for a vacation. She and her husband had gone for a yoga conference and training. It was good to talk to her again. I did not write her number down, and I lost it, so it had been another 2 years again. I knew I was always the one to call her because she was busy with family, but I did not mind, she was a great friend to me since all those years back when met in Hong Kong.

  So, I did a Google search again to find her number so I could call or leave a message at the Yoga Center. The search quickly came up with her picture and her name. I was shocked to realize I was looking at her obituary! I read it with disbelief and tears swelled up. My friend had died more than a year ago. I could not believe this.

  Overwhelmed with grief, I called my mom who had met her before, and I cried and told her about Carol passing away leaving her husband and six daughters after a courageous long battle with cancer. I could not help wondering if she knew she had cancer the last time we spoke. I tried to think what we spoke about. I remember she was subdued as we spoke but she seemed at peace with her life. I knew she had the life of her dreams, so I never worried about her.

  I read all my letters and notes from Carol and everything I could read about Carol in my mission journal, and I felt her close through my readings. I knew that she spent every one of her last moments with her most precious people—her family! I did miss her, but mostly I remembered her beautiful kind spirit always thinking of others.

I found her oldest daughter, Shanise on FACEBOOK, and I sent her a message with a few pictures I had of her mother. Her daughter told me through FACEBOOK that she was leaving on a mission to El Salvador the following week. I asked her if I could be on her email list to hear about her mission and I asked for her dad's address too. She said yes and sent me her dad's address too. I wanted to send him a card. I sent the card to her Dad with another picture of her Carol.

I still don't believe Carol is gone and that she left six beautiful daughters, the youngest was only 10. I abruptly learned through this tragic news that there is no such thing as a perfectly planned life. **The unexpected will happen.**

Chapter 47

God's perspective

It was January 2, 2013, and I was quickly heading over to my 8am appointment for the CT scan. I was thinking positive thoughts and praying that it would be a miracle and that they would find nothing at all. I knew that with perfect faith there was a power to move mountains, so I had to have positive thoughts on the outcome of my tests. I went into the office working hard to think positive about everything.

The woman at the desk said the CT scan technician was not yet there. She said that she would put in a call because the person doing my test was coming down from Show Low and the tests were normally done in the afternoon, so she was confused they had scheduled me in the morning. I was trying so hard to think only positive thoughts and keep up my faith as I waited about 20 more minutes; she finally came out and asked if I could come back in the afternoon.

I drove home disappointed that I had to psych myself up again and decided to try not to think about it anymore until right before the test, but that was really difficult to do.

Then of course, I did have a continuous prayer asking for a miracle whenever I did think about it, which was about every 5 minutes or more.

After lunch they finally called me and asked if I could come in at 12:30 pm. I left immediately and prayed for a miracle all the way there. I still had my cough and even frequently coughed almost continuously when I was lying down. So as I was lying down for the test, my cough started up again. The woman explained that I could not cough during the test and would have to not breathe at all. I asked her for some water to try to calm my cough. She left me alone with the machine turned on to get the water. I sat up and saw the red lazars that crossed against my black sweat pants. All of a sudden, I felt like time stopped, and I was mesmerized by the red beams invading my space in the quiet and sterile room. I was afraid, but I was still fighting the fear and believing I could turn it over to my Savior to fight this battle. She came back quickly with the water. I drank it and I lay back down. I told her why I was getting this test. She listened and tried not to react but was kind and she wished me good luck. I had to hold my breath a long time. Even though I did not hold it for the full count down, she said that the pictures were good so we did not have to do it over.

I asked her how long it will take to find out the results. She said about 48 hours, so maybe Friday I would know, but then again, it could be Monday. I left feeling fairly positive that things would be okay.

The next two days, I thought about Carol Harvey Stewart. I felt like this was not what I would let happen to Carol and her family. I know that I cannot see the big picture that God sees in His eternal perspective, but I am only limited to my tiny view of why things happen. This is why we need faith to get through each day, because we do not have the advantage He has of knowing the beginning from the end. To me, it is simply not right for a mother to leave before her children are raised and before she meets any of her grandchildren. Yet in reality, I am sure she met all of her, yet to be born, grandchildren when she died.

Now, I am still learning from all over again. First, she taught me how to be a missionary and how to love our investigators. Now she had taught me to appreciate life and all the blessings I do have. I will count my blessings daily. I had so far not died from cancer, even though Carol did, leaving her family to return to her Heavenly home. I don't begin to understand this, but I have peace and faith in the gospel of Jesus Christ whether I understand this or not.

I especially feel Carol's beautiful spirit through her family. A life well lived, such as Carol's, lives on through her posterity. I see the wonderful daughters she has raised with her good husband. Her amazing spirit lives on and on, and I know she will be reunited again with all of her loved ones. This is a quote from Carol in her obituary that sums up how she lived.

> "For those who wish to listen
> It is played throughout the land
> The symphony of life itself
> Directed by His hand."
> - Carol Stewart

Chapter 48

Taking care of friends

Meanwhile, I am still enjoying my good friend, Sandy, and doing whatever I can to help her survive the hardships of cancer. Sandy's hair is growing back in. I know how she feels. She recently shared with me her feelings about her hair loss and dealing with the short awkward stages as it grows back in. I fully understood her and what she is going through.

Recently on the phone, she told me she was finally not wearing her wig all the time. She told me several people have told her that her hair looked really cute; Sandy teasingly said to her friend, "Oh, you think it's cute. Hey let's cut your hair like this too. Go get the scissors, and we can do it right now." I laughed because I could relate perfectly to what she was feeling.

I am so glad Sandy is with me. I love her, and I know that her dad loves her too. In a dream, he said, "Thanks for taking care of my family." I wondered how that would happen; but now I know. Now, I have my good friend, Sandra Jill, my sister in the Gospel of Jesus Christ back, and we take care of each other.

Chapter 49

Cancer returns?

As I waited for the call that week, on the reports about my CT scan on my chest, I tried to keep busy. All my friends were praying for me. Sandy said she believed I would be alright. I hoped she was right. It was still my Christmas break, and I had plenty of time to worry. There is always something I need to do around the house, so instead, I ignored all the work and went to the temple because I needed the peace.

During the session, I listened intently during the prayer circle because I knew my name was on the temple prayer roll, and I was hoping for some message that all would be okay. As I listened that day, the officiator paused for an unusual long pause and then said, "We pray for those who are sick that they will have the courage to fight the illness." My eyes swelled up with tears.

This was not the message I hoped for. Later, in the locker room, a temple worker sister, who saw my tears after the session said "Are you okay?" She took me aside to talk. I told her everything, as my tears flowed. "I heard a message as he prayed that I think was for me. He prayed for those who are sick that they will have the courage to fight their illness." I told her, "I'm afraid the message was for me, but I have been praying for a miracle not courage to fight. I have already done that. I don't want to deal with cancer again. I am a teacher, a wife, and a step-mom. I don't want to fight this again. I don't have time too! But if I do have to, I know I will have courage because He always helps me even though I don't want too."

The tears were flowing freely as I told her this. She asked me if she could give me a hug. I hugged her and cried some more. I said,

"Thank you for the hug. I really needed a hug right now."

She said,

"If you have to do this, you can do it, and with your Heavenly Father's help. Right, you can have the courage."

I said,

"I know I can, I have done it before. If it is His will for me to have cancer, I can accept it and try to lean on Him for all things, but I hope it is not!" I left that day with the courage to fight.

The next day, we went to the temple again, and I listened again. In the prayer these words comforted me. "May our prayers be answered according to our faith and His will." I left that day knowing I had to have faith and accept His will.

It was Friday, two days after my CT scan test, and I called the Dr.'s office because it was already afternoon and thought my results were back—no phone call. He was not there, so I left a message.

He called back after about 30 minutes. "Yes I just got the test results a few minutes ago, and it says there is nothing of concern to report. There are no nodules present, not even a swollen lymph node."

My heart was leaping for joy as I listened. I knew I had had my miracle. It was His will for me to not have cancer. I was so grateful to have nothing of concern on my report. I could not wait to call all of my friends and family to report the great news! I sent this email to all my family and friends.

Dear Family and Friends,

I am so happy today because the Cat-scan showed no nodules and "nothing of concern" even though the chest X-ray showed a dense nodule. I believe all your prayers and mine were answered. I think it is safe to say that it all boils down to our faith and His will. I am pleased to say it was not His will for me to have cancer again.

Thank you! Thank you for your faithful prayers!!

> Love you all
> Nancy and Bart

Life is excellent, life is good, life is not that bad, or is it?

www.ingramcontent.com/pod-product-compliance
Lightning Source LLC
Chambersburg PA
CBHW061424040426
42450CB00007B/886